The Remainder of My Life

The Remainder of My Life

an autobiography written in real time

TROY
CARLYLE

Lulu Press

Revised Edition, 2008

Cover art and jacket design by Robert Mickey Hager

Write a review for this book. Please see the last page for details.

ISBN-978-0-6151-4439-9

For my father, who still believes in integrity.

Acknowledgements

I am deeply indebted and wish to express my gratitude to my family and friends – Mom, Carl, Todd, John, Mickey, Lynn, Sue, Shirley, Reed, Doctor Michael Borucki, and of course Zoe, who is my dog. I would like to thank especially my friends Tom Preston and James Gerardi, whose careful guidance and nurturing has shaped the revised edition.

Preface

My life, like the lives of many in the gay and lesbian community, has been marked by fear and loathing, whether self-imposed or publicly enforced. For most of my life, however, this process was of the "self-imposed" variety – fearing discovery and the associated repercussions, and loathing in myself the feelings I could not control.

Then, as I turned thirty, the reality of the temporal nature of my own physical existence caused in me a revelation – I was a mortal being. I was not getting younger, and these feelings were not, as I had hoped, going away. So I made a conscious decision to consider, for the first time, the possibility of embracing the very part of me I had before denied. I decided to see what it was like and what it meant to "be" gay.

The effect on my psyche was almost immediate. For a while, I experienced the joy of basking in the light and in the love of self-acceptance.

My joy was short-lived, however. Within weeks of coming out to myself, I became embroiled in a cruel two-year Air Force investigation that would lead to my court martial, and felt the fear and loathing of the externally imposed variety.

Gone forever was my innocence. I would never be able to recapture the freedom I had felt during those few short weeks between the onset of self-awareness and the public humiliation that followed – the unmitigated joy of self-acceptance had been replaced by a necessarily more cautious version of myself. The self that emerged from the crisis isn't, however, a sad or defeated version of my former incarnation, but rather a man more conscious of his personal call to educate and, dare I say, perhaps even inspire others.

I started work on this book in December of 2005, days after being diagnosed with AIDS. I use the acronym "AIDS" rather than the more politically correct and universal "HIV" for purposes of accuracy. "AIDS" is usually distinguished as being the symptomatic version of the more universal "HIV," which is typically asymptomatic. In other words, I was in pretty bad shape.

Other than making minor corrections and clarifying text, I resisted going back and making changes to earlier chapters, keeping the tone and content true to the time it was written. Being diagnosed with AIDS is a life-changing event, and this book remains an accurate subjective account of what I was feeling and thinking during each stage of my survival.

This book is a journal, and should be read as such, which is my way of saying that I did not set out with a grand premise or any other purpose aside from sharing my story in the hope that it might be useful to others who are sharing similar journeys or know someone who is. In other words, I didn't set out to make an argument or prove a point. While each chapter tends to explore a theme, there is no particular continuity of themes from chapter to chapter. Each day I simply sat down and wrote about whatever was on my mind. Nonetheless, I was surprised to find a theme gradually emerging as I continued to write.

In this book you will:

make a subversive film at the US Air Force Academy;

explore the wacky world of American health care;

make fresh-squeezed limeade;

shake president Reagan's hand;

meet a real modern day snake oil salesman;

be court martialed in a nationally-publicized trial,

own and manage a blues bar in North Carolina;

travel to the land of Texas and meet the Wizard of Jamieson;

discover, at age 44, the meaning of life;

and much more!!!

I have been fortunate in many ways – not the least of which is the fact I was diagnosed during the era of "protease inhibitors," the miraculous regimen of medications that means for AIDS patients an end to what was a few years ago an almost certain death sentence. At some point during my initial recovery, I sensed a change within myself – a transformation so profound as to inspire me to divide the book into parts, as you will see. This is, therefore, necessarily a book about many things. As a work inspired by a terminal illness, its pages include both hope and despair, access to and denial of health care, heartwarming acts of friendship and the pain of abandonment. It's a book about coping with the present; memories, both good and bad, from the past; and a tenuous but strengthening grasp on the future. Finally it is unavoidably and unapologetically a book about politics and religion. It may be read alternately as a journal and a series of essays -- a snapshot of today's political and religious attitudes and mores, and the effects as felt right here in the heartland. In writing a book about one, it is my hope to have written a book about and for many. I hope you enjoy reading my story.

Table of Contents

The Remainder of My Life

an autobiography written in real time

Part One: The Long Dream

Looking back, it is a simple matter to see that my first journal entries were written in a sort of fog – the fog of illness and even the fog of being near death. Far from invalidating my perception, the experience provided for me a kind of connection with the eternal – a cleansing of the perception that washed from my sight the more trivial banalities and allowed me to see loftier and more timeless issues… such as the love of friends and family and the joys of simple existence – joys expressed in the smell of rain and the taste of fresh-squeezed limeade.

Chapter 1: High Seas

I'm 45 for a moment

The sea is high

And I'm heading into a crisis

Chasing the years of my life

 -- Five For Fighting, 100 Years

AS I WRITE THIS, it's Tuesday, December 13, 2005. Less than a month ago I was diagnosed with the AIDS virus. I'm completely unfamiliar with the realities of living with AIDS, so if you're expecting an advice column, I'm afraid you've come to the wrong place. Instead, I propose a simple, straightforward and honest sharing of my experience in near real-time as it unfolds in the hope that it might be helpful to others who, like me, are new to all this. The message I would hope to relate is that I'm not alone, and neither are you.

A brief history of me includes the fact that I'm 44 years old and an Air Force veteran. After graduating from the Air Force Academy in 1984, I went on to Undergraduate Navigator Training and became a senior instructor navigator on C-130 cargo planes. I embraced my position with all the passion and patriotism of my youth, serving proudly and receiving many decorations until my court-martial in 1992 for being gay.

Beyond the inevitable local and regional news coverage, I suddenly found my deeply closeted private life on national display, as the *New York Times* and NBC's "Dateline" picked up the story, and I began to come to grips with the fact that my life would never be the same. After all, you can't be "un" outed.

As much as possible, I took the setback in stride, speaking publicly about the experience for PFLAG and other support groups and churches while making the adjustment from military to civilian life. I discovered that the worst part of being outed was also the best. With nothing to hide, even the air smelled better, and embracing the reality of who I was became a totally liberating experience. I left the closet behind and never looked back.

I've always enjoyed excellent health and count myself fortunate to have no hospitalization or even as much as a broken bone in my medical history. For a variety of reasons, I've always been fearful of sexual contact. Beyond being a little embarrassed to confess to this prudish lifestyle (think of me as the real-life "40-Year-Old Virgin"),

I've never completely understood my irrational fear. Of course, I'm not really a virgin, but suffice it to say my sexual adventures could easily be counted on my hands and feet. In any case, I make the point to help explain how anyone could endure three years of failing health before getting tested for HIV. I mean, you have to be a prolific lover to catch AIDS, don't you?

One morning in September of 2002, I woke to the symptoms of what I thought was a 24-hour flu. By early December, I was still sick; I was 7 pounds lighter and was finally persuaded to go to a clinic. The doctor chastised me for waiting so long before seeking care, announcing she had never seen a case of strep throat as bad as mine, and prescribed a course of antibiotics. As luck would have it, I suffered an adverse reaction to the prescription. By the time I showed up at a local urgent-care center a week later, I'd lost another five pounds and was so weak that it took every ounce of energy I could muster just to get there. By now, I was suffering from severe headaches, profoundly stomach-churning nausea, frequent bleeding in my stools and a sore throat brutal enough to persuade anyone that starvation was preferable to trying to ever swallow again. I couldn't have known it at the time, but as treatable as my symptoms may have been, this particular visit to urgent care was about to send me on a personal journey that would ultimately come close to killing me.

I can imagine how I must have looked when the physician walked in and closed the door. Apparently, he interpreted my emaciated state – my gaunt face, pallor and mussed hair – as a sure sign of a crack addict in search of a fix. The first thing he said –

before even asking about my symptoms – was "I'm not going to give you any narcotics."

I was numb with disbelief and too ill to be indignant. The experience took on an air of unreality. It was as if I suddenly stepped outside my own body – and I couldn't believe I was watching myself pleading for treatment, trying to convince the doctor I had not come for drugs. Without further examination, he jotted down a prescription for a different antibiotic and started to leave.

"Doctor," I said, "should I be concerned about the blood in my stool?"

With one hand on the door knob, he stopped in his tracks and let out a sigh obviously intended for my ears. "Pull your pants down," he said curtly as he closed the door with a little too much force. Without saying another word, the doctor donned a pair of disposable gloves and painfully thrust a couple of fingers into my rectum. I was in shock as I watched him remove the gloves and wash up. "There's nothing wrong with your stool," he said as he walked out the door, leaving me in total confusion. It was like being slapped in the face by a total stranger who then walks away with no explanation. I sat there for a moment in silence and remember thinking over and over, "he didn't even look at anything – I was just punished!"

Finally, the antibiotics worked. My symptoms improved and – for a while – my health returned to near normal. At night, however, my subconscious insisted on re-enacting the experience at urgent care. For the following two years, I found myself confronting the doctor again, but in my dreams I was stronger. In my dreams, I stood up for myself – sometimes I told him he shouldn't be a doctor if he hates his job so much, other times I would simply refuse to pay. In every case, I would always be filled with a profound sadness upon waking, realizing none of it was real – I had, in fact, simply let him insult and physically traumatize me. Irrationally, I resolved to avoid such humiliation again, meaning I would try to avoid doctors altogether.

My days of near-perfect health were also apparently gone for good. Every couple of months I'd miss an entire week of work and my friends expressed concern about my ongoing weight loss. On several occasions, concerned friends asked whether I'd been tested for HIV, but I assured them there was no reason. Gradually, I gave up on my business and stayed home. Days were spent in bed, then entire weeks as I tried to convince myself the whole thing was just in my head – that a positive attitude was all I needed to conquer anything.

Then I got sick again. By now, I had been unable to work for a full year… my funds had run out, so I couldn't even afford urgent care. I was so used to feeling ill that I'd forgotten what it was like to feel well. I didn't feel my situation was life-threatening, however, so a visit to the emergency room seemed inappropriate. Instead, I swallowed my pride and paid a visit to the local Social Security office.

Within a few minutes of arriving, I found myself sitting in a private cubicle with a friendly social worker who asked me a short series of questions. She discovered I had been suffering from an undetermined chronic illness, that I had no assets or means of support, that I was a childless, unmarried veteran whose benefits had been stripped, and (obviously) that I was a white male who was neither a child nor a senior citizen. As I said, she was friendly, and I understood she meant no malice when she chuckled. She was simply trying to soften the blow of her inevitable answer with a touch of humor.

Still, her laughter had hit my sense of reality in a way I hadn't anticipated. On the way home, I had to pull over for a moment. Tears streamed down my face. I had never felt so utterly alone.... I had been totally abandoned... my health, my life apparently without value. The very fact that I had even inquired about assistance merited nothing more than a dismissive laugh.

By October of 2005, my health had deteriorated to the point that my body was covered with scaly sores from my head to my feet. I suffered from relentless, ongoing nausea, and my appetite had diminished to the point that eating had become nearly impossible. One night, I remember waking up around 3:00 a.m. with an unfamiliar taste in my mouth. My eyes were burning and my skin felt as if it were on fire. It was as though every cell in my body had been replaced – I felt alien and foul, like a piece of rotting meat. I slowly peeled away my bedding, finding even the mattress and comforter saturated with perspiration. I stumbled to the bathroom and looked in the mirror.

The face staring back horrified me. For the first time I saw clearly what my friends had been trying to tell me for the previous two years – my eyes were sunken into a cartoonishly gaunt, dehydrated face, marked by deep creases in the cheeks. It was the face of a 60-year-old man. It was the face of AIDS.

By now I was freezing in the dampness of my own sweat, so I wrapped myself in a bathrobe and went online to find an anonymous, at-home HIV test.

The kit arrived a week later, though it was another week before I mustered the courage to prick my finger and send it in. In mid November of 2005, I called the 1-800 number and gave the operator my secret code. She responded with a curt, "Yeah, you're positive." Finally responding to the deadening silence from my end, the operator added, "Why? … does that surprise you?"

I went to my room and listened to the song "100 Years," by Five For Fighting. The song is about the fleeting nature of our lives. As the melody unfolded in snapshots, I considered my own life at age 15, then, 22 and 33 – and I wept, just that once, for myself. For me, that was enough self-pity. Afterwards, my attention would turn to the real victims, the family and friends my moment of indiscretion would hurt the most. I had let so many people down…. How do you tell your mom that she will likely outlive you?

My family made arrangements to drive from Texas to my home in North Carolina to take me home, along with the few personal items we could fit into their SUV. In the interim, a long line of friends began stopping by to pay their respects. Many of these hadn't visited in months, and their shocked expressions on seeing me were gut wrenching. There were tears and farewells. No one who visited me then imagined I might survive much longer. Truth be told, I wouldn't have disagreed with them.

By the time my stepfather and brother arrived, I could barely stand. Some kind of incredibly fast-growing yeast or fungus had attacked my throat, mouth and gums. It burned like acid and made eating impossible – breathing difficult. Mom called from Texas and asked my brother how I looked. Choking back his tears, he muttered a single word: "Auschwitz."

Mercifully, I slept most of the 20-hour drive to Tyler, Texas. My mom met us at the emergency room. I remember hoping the pain would stop soon, but otherwise was too "out of it" to think rationally. Forever burned into my memory, however, is the angelic face of my mother. She had endured the pain of my court martial alongside me, and it had almost killed her. Now as I gazed into her tear-filled eyes, I saw the full measure of pain I had caused. "Forgive me," was all I could say.

Everyone has heard emergency room horror stories – about excessive waits, understaffed, overworked and non-caring hospital employees – but I am happy to report just the opposite. My first visit ever to a hospital emergency room was a testament to quality care. I was seen quickly by caring professionals, and was actually feeling human again by the time I was discharged three hours later.

The following day, we had my new prescription filled, and within two days, I felt well enough to once again begin eating solid foods. Nor did the good news stop there. We discovered the Jamieson

Clinic, a public free HIV clinic, and I immediately found myself embraced by a network of wonderfully caring professionals.

Where I had felt alone and abandoned, I was suddenly worth enough to merit care, and my gratitude was and remains boundless. In a few days, I would meet my new doctor and get on a regimen that would remind me, at long last, what "feeling well" felt like. More on that as my story develops. In the meantime, I hope you all enjoyed the kind of warm, love-filled Christmas I was blessed with....

Chapter 2: Dreams

OF COURSE IT'S NOT TRUE, but we've all heard the old tale that if you die in your dreams, then you're sure to wake up dead. Oddly enough, I had such a dream shortly before my symptoms started about three years ago. It wasn't a particularly frightening experience, either. In the dream, I was a spy, a la James Bond, being chased by a team of ninjas or Russians or some other equally evil assassins – expertly dodging the bullets coming my way, when suddenly I felt the sting of a direct hit, then another, and another. As I heroically crumpled to the ground, the leader of the bad guys leaned over me and said, "You put up a good fight," which I thought was a kind of cool thing for him to say. Upon waking I was happy to realize that I remembered the dream in some detail, marveling at the mind's capacity for subconscious (and engaging) storytelling.

Some time later, I began enjoying a recurring series of dreams in which I could fly, zooming from one crisis to another, saving those unfortunate souls who had not yet learned the secret of human "lighter-than-air" propulsion techniques.

The dreams may be whimsical, but they contain a valuable lesson for all of us: We're all going to die… but that doesn't mean we can't learn to fly in the meantime. And for what it's worth, I never had another dream in which I died, but I fly almost nightly.

During my three-hour visit to the Mother Francis Emergency Room for a painful yeast infection in my throat, hospital administrators tried (understandably) to determine exactly how I intended to pay for all the truly excellent care I was receiving. After some discussion, I was told that a very helpful non-profit organization would be contacting me by phone to determine whether I was eligible for assistance. And sure enough, a few days later, they called. The friendly voice on the phone asked me three questions, discovering that I was 1) destitute, 2) disabled, and 3) dying – then apologetically but without explanation announced I wasn't eligible for assistance.

As I hung up the phone, I remembered I was now in East Texas… Bush Country. I couldn't help but imagine her response had I mentioned I was also in the oil business (I'm not). Alternately, it occurs to me that once abstinence fails, so does Bush's health care plan. There doesn't seem to be much of a back-up procedure for those of us who fail to heed the current administration's advice, which is to avoid any sexual contact whatsoever at all costs, forever and ever amen.

Then there's the Social Security Office. These understaffed, overworked dedicated professionals do their level-headed best to distribute assistance as equitably as possible. For my part, I learned volumes about American social services during my four-hour visit there. To be fair, most of this was during the final 30 minutes, after my name was finally called and I got to sit down with a social worker. Most notably, I learned that disability in this country is an all-or-none proposition. In other words, unless my doctor includes in my medical records a statement to the effect that I'm 100-percent disabled for 12 months, I get nothing. Let's say the doctor determines I'm 95-percent disabled for life – nada – no assistance. Or what if a 79.2-percent disability made me 100% unemployable? Zilch, nothing.

Don't get me wrong, either. Thanks to the Jamieson Clinic, I'll soon be getting care and there are other assistance programs I'm looking into. Still, you'll forgive me if I find humor in such unlikely events as finding myself too sick to qualify for health care.

Its amazing how quickly and how completely your values change when you find out you have AIDS. It's as though someone took

Maslow's Hierarchy[1] and turned it on its head – or at least on its side, causing much of the food, shelter & clothing nonsense to leak out. This painless process leaves plenty of room for a volume of self-actualization vastly larger than originally prescribed by Dr. Maslow. What does he know, anyway?

Where "leaving my mark" used to mean dying with lots of toys, it suddenly revolved around a sincere desire to help others. Like Ebenezer Scrooge, I'd been visited by the Ghost of Christmas Future, and the experience had changed me. Nor does the change feel particularly altruistic. I used to take pleasure in collecting rare old books, and now I take pleasure in collecting smiles. It's really no more complicated than that.

Life used to be about rushing from one destination to the next. My existence seemed to revolve around checking items off my "to do" list with rapid efficiency. The faster one can accomplish this feat (so the theory goes) the more time you'll be rewarded with to enjoy your successes. When you have AIDS, however, your destination comes into sharp focus and seems much nearer than you imagined. Paradoxically, you become less concerned about rushing toward a destination and far more interested in appreciating the journey. If you find it difficult to understand this idea, I suggest you observe children at play. We can learn much from them.

---

[1] Abraham Maslow (1908-1970), American psychologist noted for proposing a "Hierarchy of Human Needs," suggesting that people will seek shelter only after they have satisfied the need for food, etc.

I used to be an amateur filmmaker, even had the great honor of teaching college film and video classes at an art school in Houston for a few years. I was always fascinated with "color temperature," the phenomenon of the changing color of sunlight as it shifts from a relatively cool reddish tint in the morning to the warmer hues of blue before returning to the fiery shades of reds and oranges at sunset[2]. In those days, I was mesmerized by the science behind all this, but now, like a child full of wonder, I find myself seeing this magic for the first time. Every morning I watch as the light show begins, dramatically transforming the grey trees into brilliant shades of orange. The noonday sky, I find, is sometimes so clear and deeply blue as to inspire a kind of poetry of the soul (the only type of poetry afforded to non-poets like me).

Recently, I read an inspirational article by a young man who's been living with the virus for some ten years now. He was writing about how his disease had changed his values, made him more fearless… willing to take chances his pre-HIV self would never have risked. For him, the change was so marvelously profound he added that, at this point in his life, he wouldn't give up the virus even if he could. While I can now understand, even appreciate, his sentiment, you'll forgive me if I chuckle a little as I freely admit I'd prefer to be

---

[2] It's true! While we normally think of "reddish" tints as warmer than the "bluish" ones (subtractive color process), it works just the opposite with light (additive color process). Bluish light therefore has a higher color temperature (warmer) than its reddish (cooler) cousin.

healthy. I'd prefer to regain about 25 pounds, not to be constantly nauseous, not to require 14 hours of sleep daily, not to get dizzy every time I stand, not to be covered with sores, not to be a burden or constant cause of concern for my family and friends. But then, today is New Year's Eve, 2005. Tomorrow starts a brand new year, full of promise, and starts my final five days of waiting to meet my doctor and begin treatment.

For now, let's just say I'm thankful to be alive, thankful to be loved, thankful for each brilliant sunrise, and especially thankful that I can still dream of flying. That's one dream I wish for all of you.

Chapter 3: Limeade and Salsa

When I was a child, I would make promises to myself about the person I intended to grow up to be. These promises were often inspired by miraculous personal experiences I never wanted to forget or, more frequently, by the stuffy behavior of adults who seemed to take no pleasure in their own lives and for whom observing children take pleasure in theirs had become an exercise in unbearable pain.

Here are a few examples of promises from the child I was to the adult I've become:

When I grow up, I'll let kids laugh as loud as they want to for as long as they want. Even if I'm reading the newspaper or watching some dumb TV show, I'll always remember that laughter is lots more important than bad news and dumb TV shows.

When I grow up I'll never turn down a child who asks me to play. There's nothing in the world quite so special as the amazement on a child's face when I show them how to build a toy gun out of Legos that actually shoots Lego bullets... and not one of these children to date has translated their fascination with Lego guns into a life of crime. If the child becomes so inspired by my Lego construction as to suddenly require *all* the blocks I was using, then I've helped to spark some real creativity. When I grow up I'll never get jealous and throw a tantrum because he or she took my blocks. After all, I'm supposed to be the adult.

When I grow up I'll never let my taste buds get old. Everyone knows that Fruit Loops & Crunchberries taste lots better than dumb old bran flakes. Yuck!

Forgive my digression, but I suppose all this has been my way of getting around to flavors. For some reason, my illness has brought out in me a joyous appreciation for some of the delectable concoctions from my childhood. These taste sensations, while absurdly simple to make, seem to have been lost in the expertly distracting supermarket aisles and deceptively attractive packaging. It seems all you need nowadays is a microwave, and you can produce a delicious bowl of Olestra-seasoned melted plastic before your family has time to say "What's for dinner?"

I'm no chef, so I'm going to keep this real simple (simpler yet, since Grandma's recipe for homemade egg noodles has been lost to posterity).

Child labor laws serve an important purpose, I suppose, yet I counted myself fortunate to land my first job as an executive car hop at the ripe old age of 13 at my favorite restaurant – A&W. While the best part of the job was a wonderful manager and a handsome weekly paycheck computed at 95 cents per hour (65 cents after taxes), the best perk was getting all the root beer (served in frosty mugs) my adolescent heart desired. I worked there for over a year, and never got tired of frosty mugs of root beer. Mmmmm.

Our restaurant was also famous for its fresh-squeezed limeade and (oddly enough) tacos made with home-made salsa. Accordingly, one of the promises my child self made to my adult self was to commit to memory two top-secret and proprietary recipes: Fresh Limeade and Homemade Salsa. These highly sought-after secrets remained locked tightly away and untested in the recesses of my mind for 30 years – neither disclosed nor even privately produced until a few days ago, when an event of near tragic proportions inspired me to break a time-honored promise to my beloved first employer.

In order to keep the lawyers at bay, I'll omit the name of the restaurant, but let's just say I stopped by a local drive-in (Sonic) that advertised "fresh-squeezed limeade." It had been years since I'd tasted a real limeade (no offense intended to the Crystal Light Corp. or the friendly folks at Kool-Aid), and so it was with near breathless anticipation I gently cradled my beverage in the cup-holder as mom drove us home.

Settling into a comfortable chair, I raised the supersize Styrofoam cup to my lips and tasted…. "Surely there was some mistake," I thought. So I tried another sip. To my dismay, the Sonic employee had apparently produced my "fresh-squeezed limeade" by dropping a microscopically thin slice of lime into a cup of 7-Up. This is ridiculous for two reasons – 1) presumably due to the intense amount of extra labor required to squeeze a slice of lime, Sonic charges a premium for this beverage – significantly higher than a prefabricated soda; and 2) as a former A&W executive limeade chef, I happen to know the "labor myth" is just that... a myth. There's nothing in the world, save ice water, easier to make. As long as you promise to keep our secret safe, here are the recipes for fresh-squeezed limeade & fresh homemade salsa. Once you try them, I guarantee you'll never buy the pre-fabricated versions again.

Fresh Squeezed Limeade (by the glass)

You will need:

1 quart of water, in a sauce pan

Sugar

1 lime can make up to 3 12-oz servings

Your choice of unflavored carbonated soda water or the simple filtered (uncarbonated) kind. I prefer soda water because it adds a tingly zing and has a calming effect on my (frequently nauseated) stomach

Ice – cold is best, though if you're sensitive, you can use the melted variety. I'll include a short section on how to melt ice in my next chapter.

Directions: The only real prep work for limeade is making the simple syrup. This only takes a few minutes and it will stay fresh a few days in a refrigerator. The idea behind simple syrup is simple chemistry. While cool water is quickly saturated by sugar, hot water can "hold" much more. The real magic here is that, even when cooled, the saturated simple syrup holds on to the sugar you dissolved while it was hot. This makes an excellent sweetener without which, for example, true Southern sweet tea would be impossible. There's no real secret to making simple syrup. Just heat a quart of water on the stove & add gobs of sugar. Stir 'till completely dissolved, then allow to cool and package for storage.

Fill a tall glass ¾ full of ice and add your soda water (or the uncarbonated type, if you prefer) just to the top of the ice.

Cut your lime into 1/8 wedges, and fiercely squeeze 3 of these (more or fewer to taste) over the top. There should be plenty of pulp floating in the glass as you drop each expended wedge into the glass.

Drizzle your simple syrup over the top, stirring and tasting till you determine your preference (Caution: there's nothing quite as sad as an overly-sweetened limeade. Like salt, it's a lot easier to add more than it is to remove).

That's it! Even if you're making your initial batch of syrup, the whole process takes no longer than five minutes or so… and the results are magic.

Homemade Salsa

You will need

Tomatoes – 3 or 4 large, juicy, flavorful tomatoes. If the tomatoes at your grocer are flavorless orange water balloons, may I suggest your local farmer's market.

Onion – sweet Vidalia onions are best. In fact, if you can't get sweet Vidalia onions, I would suggest you consider leaving out the onion altogether (yeah, it's that important). Caution: my HIV has made me very sensitive to raw onion. If this describes you, here are two ideas you might want to try: 1) where I used to use a whole onion, I now add only a few slivers for flavor; 2) you might also consider sautéing the onion first. Sautéing, for most people, renders the onion tummy-safe, allowing you to add as much as you like, up to one whole onion. As for me, I prefer the raw, crunchy version, so I use option 1.

Green pepper (optional) I just like the color a green pepper imparts, along with a flavor best described as "freshness incarnate." This is the only ingredient I've added to the original A&W version. I typically add only a sliver, fearing a whole green pepper might excessively alter the flavor.

Jalapeno (fresh, not pickled) At least one whole jalapeno will be needed. My sensitive stomach will allow no more than that, though my taste buds still yearn for more. Feel free to add as much or little as you like.

Salt is another seasoning I've had to cut back on. My HIV-affected taste buds seem to have become hyper-sensitive to relatively small doses of salt. Still, some salt is vital. Just add it slowly and stop when you hit the "delicious" zone that's right for you.

Lime (optional) – as both a preservative and a flavor enhancer, consider squeezing one of the lime slices you have left over from your limeade into your batch of the best salsa you ever tasted.

Cilantro – to taste. Most of the flavor comes from the leaves, so consider discarding the stems.

Depending on the consistency you prefer, you will also need a blender or a food processor – blender for a smooth salsa, food processor for a chunkier variety.

Directions: (this is the best part). Without any excessive slicing or dicing of anything (that's why God invented blenders) start by cutting out and discarding any parts you'd prefer not to eat. For example, tomato stems and jalapeno stems are stringy and bland – I recommend you remove them. Most chefs also remove the inside part of green peppers. The jalapeno seeds I leave to your discretion (I like them, but be aware they tend to add some additional "heat").

Your prep work complete, toss everything into a blender (or processor) and blend at a slow speed for a few seconds.

Ta-da! Pour and serve.

My illness has awakened in me a strong preference for fresh flavors and healthy-tasting foods. My sense of taste seems to have been altered to the point that I can taste the chemicals in many pre-prepared foods. Add the fact that fresh, homemade concoctions can actually be easier to make, less expensive, and much healthier, and you have a recipe for a healthy new menu that's far more delicious than its pre-fabricated cousins.

Tomorrow is my first visit to My HIV doctor, so I plan to focus on health care and my experience at the clinic next. In the meantime, I'll leave you with something funny that happened to me a couple of days ago.

I love my mom, but she can often be hilarious without even trying. My mom is pretty spiritual and is always sharing inspirational tidbits she gets at church or by email. The other morning she handed me a wonderful list of affirmations reminding people how to live a happy, well adjusted life. Toward the bottom of the page, she had carefully highlighted, in green marker, the zinger intended to help me. It read: "JUST FOR TODAY, I will do something positive to improve my health. If I'm a smoker, I'll quit."

I do intend to get some help from my doctor to quit smoking, but this struck me as funny for two reasons. Firstly, that I presumably had no idea, 'till reading the affirmation, that smoking might be bad for me; and secondly, there was the (un-highlighted) sentence immediately preceding the one about smoking. It read: "JUST FOR TODAY: I'll refrain from improving anybody but myself."

Apparently, Mom didn't feel that one applied to her.

I don't care who you are, that there's funny!

Chapter 4: The Wizard of Jamieson: A Play in Three Acts

The Cast:

The Scarecrow: One of the most caring people I've met at Jamieson (which says volumes), she is a Nurse of some 30 years and my main point of contact there. I chose Scarecrow for her character after remembering a line from the movie, when Dorothy is recounting her dream and says to Scarecrow, "I loved you most of all." Best qualities: infinite patience and she laughs at my jokes. Worst quality: absolutely none.

The Cowardly Lion: A character I met in the waiting room. You just can't make this kind of material up. She's a real gem... once you get past the fact that you're gonna end up in a conversation with her no matter how concerted your efforts to avoid it. Best qualities: she'll most likely never fully comprehend how hilarious she is, and she is surprisingly capable of amazingly engaging conversation. Worst quality: she is also amazingly capable of spewing utter nonsense. When everything is said and done, she simply keeps on talking.

The Tin Man: A nurse practitioner who either A) was having a bad day; B) doesn't realize he already has a heart; or C), and most likely, both A and B above. He's one of those expressionless professionals, not much into small talk. Still, there's an intangible, endearing quality about him that made him instantly likeable – a Texan brand of gruffness that requires no further proof of genuine kindness than the fact that he's too much of a Texan to express it. Best qualities: professionalism combined with a caring, gentle and respectful technique. He is also rust-proof. Worst quality: failure to laugh at my jokes.

The Good Witch of the North, Glenda: My mom has suffered from long-term clinical major depression for decades now, which makes her ability to be an excellent and loving caregiver all the more miraculous. Best quality: her loving and tireless devotion to my needs. Worst quality: her loving and tireless devotion to my needs.

The Wicked Witch of the West and her army of flying monkeys: played expertly by my new constant companions – the little HIV guys rapidly reproducing in my bloodstream.

Toto: Played by Zoe, a black Lab / Pit mix (I believe this makes her a full-bred Pitrador) who sleeps with me and without whose constant companionship over the past three years, I would likely not have retained enough sanity to be able to write my name, let alone books. Her marvelous capacity to warm the spirit has also earned her the nickname "Dog Blanket." When our heater went out in North Carolina, for example, she would lay on top of me with her muzzle against my cheek. She wanted to make sure I was warm enough. She makes no further appearance in our production.

The Wizard: My doctor graduated from the University of Texas Medical Branch in 1983, followed by a residency specializing in infectious diseases. In other words, he was on the scene practically since day one of the AIDS pandemic. He is also a teacher, and is well known, liked and respected throughout the region. Finally, he has been instrumental in helping to develop new HIV therapies and drug regimens. Beyond that, I found him highly likeable – inspiring trust and showing great concern for his patients. Best quality: medical prowess aside, it takes a tremendous amount of love to be a good teacher. I respect that. Worst quality: the poor guy is stuck with me as a patient, meaning I'll be quite literally hanging on to him for dear life. Sorry, dude.

Dorothy: That would be me. Fortunately for you, at no point in this production will I attempt to sing. Unfortunately for you, I look ridiculous in a dress. Now if you'll excuse me, it's curtain call and these ruby-red slippers aren't going to polish themselves.

Act I: Dorothy finds herself in the Land of Jamieson

Shortly after the house fell on me, I found myself sitting with my brother in the cozy waiting room at the Jamieson Free Clinic for HIV & AIDS in Tyler, Texas. It was Dec 11, 2005. About a week prior, my brother and stepfather had driven to Wilmington, NC to deliver all 140 lbs that were left of me back home for care and convalescence.

After a few minutes, my nurse (the Scarecrow in our play) brought me back to her office and conducted a thorough interview called an "intake." There was lab work to be done and many questions regarding symptoms and sexual history.

At one point she paused dramatically, announcing that there were three very important rules that must be adhered to at all times. Assured by my grave attention, she began:

"Firstly, if there is an emergency, go to a hospital emergency room, not here. We don't treat emergencies here."

"Secondly, if there is an emergency, go to a hospital emergency room, not here. We don't treat emergencies here."

"And finally, if there is an emergency, go to a hospital emergency room, not here. We don't treat emergencies here."

She asked me whether I had fully comprehended and I nodded as her attention returned to the thick stack of paperwork we still had to complete. "Umm," I said, as her eyes expertly glanced upward in such a way that all the remaining muscles in her head and neck remained firmly focused on the paperwork as if to say "Don't you dare--."

"Umm," I repeated, "what if I have an emergency...?"

She fought it valiantly, but the smile that started at the corners of her mouth gradually crept across her face, and I knew I was gonna like Scarecrow just fine.

As the extensive interview progressed, we inevitably arrived at the section regarding my sexual proclivity. "Have you ever had sex with a woman?" she queried.

Reaching into the deepest recesses of my memory, I answered truthfully: "Yes," I said, "but I was young and didn't know any better."

Perhaps softened by her previous close encounter with a near chuckle, Scarecrow nearly fell off her chair. She was laughing – and that made her instantly dear in my book. I had a friend at Jamieson, and that felt pretty good.

Act II: The Yellow Brick Road

My follow-up visit to Jamieson was tinted with an entirely different atmosphere. The waiting room was crowded with patients pretending to read various pharmaceutical brochures. The silence was deafening.

It was a different story on the other side of the glass, as well. This area was abuzz with a staff of near-frantic nurses, seemingly on the verge of being overwhelmed. When I checked in at the window, Scarecrow simply asked me to take a seat, amazing me again that she did this without either looking up or interrupting her instructions to another nurse, who was being directed toward her next set of duties.

I sat down with my step-dad and pretended to read a pharmaceutical brochure. My step-dad was disappointed that there were no golfing magazines in the entire building – not even for golfers with AIDS. I offered him an article about bowlers with AIDS, but he wasn't much interested. "It's not really the same, is it?" he snipped.

Enter the Cowardly Lion – which is really a stretch, since she was neither cowardly nor lion-like. Still, like the Cowardly Lion, her initial "roar" quickly gave way to a softer (if somewhat disturbed) demeanor.

She was a slender woman whose creased face and brittle, stringy hair left little clue to her age, aside from the appearance that she spent a lot of time outdoors. Somewhere between 40 and 60 would be my guess.

The sliding glass window between the waiting room and the nurse's station had been closed, which left a thin strip of countertop not quite wide enough to support the remainder of Lion's partially eaten McCheeseburger, which promptly flopped onto the floor. Without missing a beat, she simply picked it up and took another bite.

Tiny bits of moist bread & burger gently sprayed against the glass as she began: "Look," she hollered in the general direction of the soundproof window, "you people gave me trichinosis!"

Apparently not entirely soundproof. Scarecrow stopped mid-sentence and turned toward Lion. With some visible trepidation and in slow motion, she opened the window just a crack. "Excuse me?" She said.

"I have AIDS and was here two weeks ago for lab work and you were supposed to test me for trichinosis and you obviously didn't 'cause I have it and thanks to you so does my boyfriend."

Scarecrow whispered, "That's something you should tell the doctor privately. That's very personal information and we try to protect your privacy here. There's no need for these people in the waiting room to know your business."

When Lion swung around to face the waiting room, I guarantee the great John Wayne himself couldn't have done it with more swagger.

"And why is that?" She was addressing us now. "We're all here for the same reason, right? We all have AIDS, right?"

Of course, she was right, though most of us certainly weren't in the mood to discuss it with a stranger (certainly not with a stranger as strange as this one).

Accordingly, the entire waiting room became a synchronized swimming team, simultaneously covering our eyes with one hand and diving headlong into what had just become the most fascinating pharmaceutical literature ever written. Mine was about uncontrollable and frequent liquid bowel movements.

"I mean," Lion continued as she sat next to my step-dad, "what would you do?" I kept wondering who she was talking to, but couldn't look for fear it might be me. "I come in here and they don't test me for trichinosis like they're supposed to. Next thing I know, I give it to my boyfriend and he gives it to his wife."

Thank God I'm a smoker, because at this point, I was in desperate need of an excuse to seek out a private place to let loose the healthiest belly laugh I'd enjoyed in weeks.

By the time I returned from my smoke, much of the waiting room had been cleared out. There remained only an attractive young girl, sitting quietly in the corner, my step-dad and Lion, who had apparently not paused from her monologue long enough to take a breath. My step-dad must have momentarily glanced up from his brochure, because all her attention was now focused squarely at him. My poor step-dad. Aside from an occasional nod or half-smile, he couldn't have inserted a comma with a gas-powered log-splitter.

Suddenly, two Texas Department of Corrections officers burst onto the scene with a young woman in tow, stylishly attired in a blue smock, cuffs and shackles. No sooner had they sat down than another patient entered, then another and another – each new arrival providing another listener for Lion, who was now telling a story about finding an unusually shaped button while walking near a beach somewhere.

My appointment time had come and gone… was now in the hour-and-a-half late category. From time to time I'd hear, over the din of Lion's monologue, someone quietly complain that their appointment was supposed to be fifteen minutes ago, putting them at risk of rearranging their whole daily schedule. For my part, I was thankful to have a facility like Jamieson available. It seemed a bit absurd to me to complain that my free medical care wasn't expeditious enough for my taste. And as for rearranging my schedule, I couldn't imagine what might be more important. "Wheel of Fortune" was a re-run-anyway.

The waiting room had emptied once again. Even Lion had been mercifully called into the clinic recesses, along with "prisoner person." My appointment was now three hours past due, and I didn't mind, except for the inconvenience to my step-dad. But he's always had the patience it took me a truckload of flying monkeys to master. "Don't worry," he said calmly, "I'm here with you for as long as it takes."

"By the way," he added, "are you finished with that brochure about uncontrollable frequent liquid bowel movements?"

"Yeah," I said, "and I think there's a golfer in it too."

Then the window slid open and a smiling face called my name. "Dorothy," she said, "you can come back now."

She didn't really call me "Dorothy."

I met Tin Man in one of the small, private examination rooms. He was tall and slim, dressed in a white smock, about 50 years old, and announced flatly that he was a Nurse Practitioner, which made me wonder briefly whether the other nurses were so authorized to actually "practice" nursing.

He told me he was to conduct a procedure on me called a "penile swab," and cautioned that it would be "uncomfortable," but only for a "short period of time."

My head swam with fear. "Penal swab." That sounded like something you do on the deck of a prison ship. I was sweating bullets as he mechanically donned a pair of unpowdered surgical gloves.

"Do you have any discharge?" he asked.

Discharge? I wondered silently. It's a penis! I pondered, of course I have discharge! Wouldn't you eventually explode? How should I answer?

So I formulated a response as specific and honest as I could: "Only when it's on purpose," I said.

The moment I uttered those words, I realized how funny I must have sounded. But Tin Man remained frighteningly expressionless. "Pull down your pants," he ordered.

My whole body shook with fear and my teeth were clenched tight enough to chip. When I saw Tin Man dip the end of a Q-Tip into a translucent oily substance, I nearly fainted.

"Hold perfectly still," he said, his expressionless voice barely audible over the screaming in my head that kept repeating "Run!!!! Run while you still can!!!!"

A slight cold sensation as a latex glove steadied my fear-shrunken member for "penal swabbing," followed by the gentlest, least obtrusive swabbing I could have ever wished for. The whole procedure had taken less than five seconds and, while not pleasant by any means, had certainly been utterly painless.

"That's it," he said dryly, "please have a seat in waiting room two."

"Thank you," I offered. Then, realizing how stupid that must have sounded, added, "for being gentle," which only made me feel more ridiculous.

He just stared at me gravely as if to say, "What part of 'have a seat in waiting room two' are you having trouble with?"

As I approached waiting room two, Lion was just leaving, shouting obscenities over her shoulder at another female patient, who by now was in full fight stance and saying, "Why don't you come here and say that?"

Once again, the synchronized swim team leapt into action, chanting in unison, "Let her go… its not worth going back to prison."

"BACK?" I asked myself. Had they said "*Back* to prison?" And had the other patients known her there? How else would they know she had been a prisoner? It's worthy of mentioning that "prisoner girl" and her police escorts were not involved in the fray. Different woman, different fight.

The mantra continued as I, caught up in the spirit of the moment, joined in: "It's not worth it… It's not worth it," we repeated.

Lion left without incident and I sat next to the most normal-looking patient I could find – who happened to be the young, attractive girl I'd seen hours earlier in waiting room one.

"Pretty crazy stuff, huh?" I offered.

"Yeah," she said. "But it's cool. I have my last visit with my parole officer tomorrow, then I get to spend more time with my horses."

I simply smiled and grabbed a brochure (which I discovered several minutes later was upside down). Apparently, this was "inmate day" at the clinic.

Suddenly, Scarecrow appeared and apologetically informed me I could go. "You shouldn't have been sent to waiting room two," she said.

Intermission

The moral of Act II, I suppose, has something to do with humility, patience and thanks. I couldn't help but smile as my step-dad and I exited the clinic (stage right). I felt thankful for a staff of professionals with the patience to deal with unruly mobs of some of the most adorably odd characters I'd ever met. Then I thought of Tin Man – what a job he has! I wouldn't want to be the guy in charge of penal swabs, no sir. And God bless the guy who stands up to accept that important duty with the kind of careful, quiet professionalism he does. Who cares if I had to wait three hours for a five-second procedure. Life is an adventure, and I'm part of it. Thank goodness I set the VCR to record "Wheel of Fortune."

Please stop by our concession booth in the lobby – lots of tasty treats to tide you over while we prepare the scenery for the third and final act of our play: The Beige City and the Wizard of Jamieson.

Chapter 5: The Wizard of Jamieson: Act III

FUNNY HOW FAST PEOPLE GET RELIGIOUS when they get sick. Well, I guess I'm no exception, so here goes:

Dear God, I have spent my life completely self-absorbed. Where I used to fear failure and personal embarrassment, I now fear failure to leave a lasting legacy. Where I used to seek out personal comfort, I now seek out the gift of being able to help someone…anyone. Let me help, please? Just enough time to make a difference to someone, that's all I need from you. I'm not worried about pain or discomfort, but I grow weary; I just need a little more strength… a little more time. There is much to be done… (to be continued)

Act III: The Beige City and the Wizard of Jamieson

In our play, my journey down the Yellow Brick Road started when I arrived in Tyler, Texas and lasted just over a month. A month from my first visit to the emergency room with a near-fatal bout of thrush – a month of applying for aid, lab work and generally jumping through all the hoops required to get into "the system." Along the way, I met some interesting characters – Scarecrow, Lion and Tin Man. In reality, however, this journey began some three years earlier when I first came down with what I thought was the flu. Remaining undiagnosed until November 2005 also meant remaining untreated. My health gradually failed. I had forgotten what wellness felt like, but the Wizard was going to change all that. When I walked into Jamieson I found myself in a land of possibilities – a gleaming beige city I had worked so hard to reach. The Wizard had granted me an audience. "By tomorrow," I allowed myself to imagine, "I will start to feel better."

The waiting room was eerily empty and silent when I arrived, the ghosts of the many characters from my previous visit firmly planted in their chairs, pretending to read their brochures. I kinda missed Lion.

I had an early morning appointment and waited just 15 minutes before my name was called. The Wizard entered the exam room before I had a chance to sit down, firmly shaking my hand and introducing himself.

"I am the Great and Powerful Wizard of Jamieson," he announced into a microphone as cherubs sang and munchkins

scurried about, orchestrating the impressive smoke and light show….
Scratch that. He just walked in and shook my hand.

He was about my age and full of energy – eyes shining with optimism. I felt better already.

He started to explain that he had a couple of students with him, but I stopped him mid-sentence. "Please invite them in," I said. I was in a hurry for the magic pills, and didn't need to be sold on the value of training new doctors.

The Wizard just smiled and waved in two male students. "God, they're young," I thought. Or maybe I was just getting old.

First, we went over my symptoms -- heartburn and nausea, sleeplessness, sores, scales, itching, pain, fatigue, sweats, dizziness -- and then he conducted a physical exam. He wrote entire paragraphs in my record just describing the many varieties of lesions on my body. He had more ways to describe sores than the Eskimos have to describe snow. At one point, I jokingly accused him of making them up as he went.

"Now," he said, "let's talk about your lab work."

"First," he announced, pointing to the lab report, "you should know you have had hepatitis B."

The students watched in fascination as my lower jaw gently scraped the floor.

He explained that aside from some slight liver damage, there were no further risks associated with the disease. "You no longer have it," he added, "and the fact that you did have it makes you immune from ever getting it again. Furthermore, you tested negative for hepatitis C, which is a far more severe disease."

Of course, I would have preferred never to have had hepatitis, but I decided to accept the "immunity" part as a good thing.

The Wizard then sat on the edge of the examination table and looked me square in the eyes. "Now we come to the meat of your lab report. I'm sure you've done a lot of reading by now on HIV and the many available treatments."

I shrugged non-committally. The fact of the matter is that, between my failing eyesight and the rapidly changing landscape of treatment options, I had read very little – aside from discovering that T-Cells were now more commonly referred to as "CD-4" cells.

The Wizard carefully circled a number on the lab report and said, "This is your CD-4 count."

The number was "94." (1,400 is considered normal.)

"Now we can get that number back up," he said, "but its going to take some time. In the meantime, you need to understand that, between your CD-4 count, facial wasting and other symptoms, we would call this full-blown AIDS."

Directing my attention back to the report, The Wizard continued: "This section shows your viral load, which counts the amount of the virus in your bloodstream, and yours is off the chart, meaning there's too much virus in your bloodstream for us to accurately measure."

My heart sank, dreams of "recovery" and "wellness" rapidly fading.

"We're going to get you healthier," he reassured, "but it's going to take some time, and it's important you maintain a positive mental attitude."

"There are many treatment options we can discuss, but the fact that the disease in your case is so advanced, combined with the fact that you haven't yet received any treatment, could make you an excellent candidate for clinical trials."

I raised my palm to stop the clinical-trial sales pitch. "Doctor," I said, "this disease has affected me physically in many ways, but the most profound change in me has been spiritual. If you're telling me I have an opportunity to help others by helping to develop better treatment options -- to create a legacy -- I'm your man."

He explained that preparing for the trial would cause a delay in my treatment. We would need to establish a baseline through further testing. It would take two weeks to get into the program, then another week before getting my magic pills.

I'd rather be well, but my spirit rose at the thought of doing some good, and that's pretty good medicine, too.

***

That was yesterday, and my first visit with the Wizard of Jamieson. But now, in the early morning hours of a new day, my thoughts return to this prayerful notion that time itself is short....

I love carnivals and fairs, but it struck me recently that I've only ridden the merry-go-round two or three times in my entire life. As a child, I was quickly drawn to rides far faster, scarier, bigger, better. The merry-go-round, after all, is for little kids, and who wants to be a little kid? Somehow I never made it back to the place it all started, the merry-go-round.

Eventually, the Zipper and the tilt-a-whirl struck me as more stomach-churning and migraine-producing endeavors than fun. I was growing up. Then, I loved the carnival for the overpriced food and absurd games, carefully rigged to make winning a keychain nearly impossible, let alone the stuffed animals displayed on the backdrop. I'm convinced the carnies must hire people to walk through the crowd carrying large stuffed animals for the sole purpose of convincing the rest of us that the impossible is, in fact, possible

Now, it seems my love affair with the carnival isn't about bigger, faster rides, tasty treats or even stuffed animals – it's about the merry-go-round, and always has been. I suppose I just need to know it's there, need to see it – and recall (after far too few actual rides) that wondrous feeling of riding a plaster horse in circles.

The merry-go-round looks deceptively boring. Still, you're kind of excited to find your favorite horse vacant. You climb up – way up, because it's a big horse – and wait for the ride to fill. Children scurry to find their favorite horses, and one child begins to cry because his choice has been taken. "Poor kid," you think as you sit smugly on your horse, thankful that you're not the one who has to ride the elephant.

The ride begins with a slight jerk, which produces on your face the widest grin humanly possible. "Here we go!" you think. You hold tight to the pole as the ride reaches full speed, which is much, much faster than it appeared from the queue. Now you're being thrust though the world at breakneck speeds, up and down, round and round, the wind on your face reaching gale force.

The world is a blur and the music fills not only your ears, but your entire body. You *feel* it. You are on a time machine – an adventure. Nothing else exists. You are timeless and without concern for anything but the sound of your own laughter.

Then, far too soon, the ride begins to slow. You try to convince yourself its your imagination -- that the operator will give you just another minute or two – but now it's clear the dream is ending. As the ride continues to slow you try to go back to the imaginary land, but the moment has passed. No longer a blur, the world comes back into focus, bringing with it thoughts of school and homework and other burdens of childhood.

How could I have forgotten all this for so long? Please, Mr. Operator, I'd like to ride the merry-go-round one more time – and there's another ticket in it for you if you'll give me an extra minute or two.

A few years ago, I took Daniel, the one true love of my life, to an amusement park. He loves dolphins, so we were drawn to a game with huge stuffed dolphins hanging from the backdrop. I threw a handful of rings onto a handful of bottles, and I'll be damned if I didn't win one of those dolphins for him. As we walked through the crowd, arms around each other, I thought to myself, "Maybe the impossible isn't so impossible after all."

Chapter 6: Another Day in Paradise

Waltzing matilda, waltzing matilda Who'll come a waltzing matilda with me? And he sang as he watched and waited 'til his billy boiled. Who'll come a-waltzing matilda with me?
-- with apologies to 'Banjo' (A.B.) Patterson, c. 1890

TODAY IS JANUARY 12, 2006. Yesterday began with an early-morning visit to the University of Texas Medical Center for screening to get into a pharmaceutical research program administered by GlaxoSmithKline (GSK).

Yesterday was not a good day.

My condition seems to be deteriorating. What used to be constant nausea became acute painful stomach cramps that hit me with the force of a pro-football tackle every time I swallow solid food (and for hours thereafter). My night-sweats now wake me up at regular intervals of 1½ hours. As I write, it's 6:00 a.m. and I'm wearing the fourth set of pajama bottoms I've had to don since going to bed last night... the fourth pair of underwear... the fourth t-shirt. And thankfully, I'm on a queen-sized bed, since I need to switch sides every time I wake in order to avoid lying back in a chilling pool of my own sweat.

I suffer from the sensation of painful random needle jabs, causing me to jerk and wince from time to time – irritating by day, but absolutely exasperating at night.

Then there's my skin, the many sores and lesions forming a delightful challenge for connect-the-dot fans.

The most frightening new symptom is all in my head. I find myself having difficulty forming some words, my speech is slower, my short-term memory failing, and (horror!) I occasionally drool from the corners of my mouth.

As a former USAF officer, then as a business owner and employer, I'm accustomed to a level of quiet respect – at least a modicum of personal dignity. Yet, while I've only been in Texas with my family for a month and a half, the days in North Carolina flee rapidly toward the dark recesses of memory. It seems like years since those days. Now I find myself increasingly needful of help, increasingly stooped, less able to concentrate, more likely to... wow, I just forgot what I was going to say (no joke).

The point being, I was already having a bad day when I showed up for my appointment at the University of Texas (UT) Medical Center, which has been oddly placed off a freeway, several miles outside of Tyler, amidst construction companies and purveyors of farming implements.

You may recall meeting the "Wizard of Jamieson" in our previous chapter. His real name is Dr. Michael Borucki. His main office is at UT Medical Center, right alongside the Pharmaceutical Research Dept., which is where I was to report.

I was warmly greeted by a tall woman, who ushered me into a cluster of offices and exam rooms. Safely cloistered in one of these rooms, she began to read pages of required material on the topic of "informed consent." While this exercise promised to be dull, I quickly found myself mesmerized – like a child hearing a bedtime story – at the turn of each phrase. It occurred to me that this was no ordinary contract… it was a matter of life or death.

This was to be a double-blind study, meaning no one at this site, medical staff or patient, would know which drugs I'd be taking. The experiment will compare the efficacy of two commonly prescribed (and FDA-approved) HIV medications: Epzicom and Truvada. The "FDA-approved" part was reassuring.

The patients in the study are given both Epzicom and Truvada, though one of these is replaced by a placebo. Furthermore, the placebo looks identical to the real McCoy so that even the doctor won't know which drug I'm actually receiving – which is why they call it "double blind."

Of course, "FDA-approved" should not be read as "safe," as I discovered when we got to the list of side effects. One paragraph on the topic of "hypersensitivity reaction" got my attention when the attendant read: "This reaction can be life threatening and in rare cases has been fatal," which seemed rather redundant to me – I mean… what's the difference between "life threatening" and "in rare cases has been fatal?" While I can live with the risk of "rare cases," I was concerned when I learned the list of symptoms, 95 percent of which I already have! In other words, there would be precious few indicators that I might suddenly perish from hypersensitivity reaction.

"What the hell," I thought… "I have the same odds outside the study, since I could be prescribed the same drug anyway." Besides, the informed-consent form made clear my right to withdraw at any time, and seemed generally liberal with its interpretation of patients' rights.

The best part was my discovery that Dr. Borucki would be conducting the research – meaning he would be both my primary caregiver at Jamieson Clinic and my doctor at UT Medical Center.

After The Reading and The Signing of the Documents, it was time for The Weighing, The Urine Sampling and The Taking of the Blood, all of which went smoothly… until the blood part. In my emaciated state it seems my blood vessels have become harder to find and, once located, harder to keep inflated enough to draw the required six test tubes of blood. Still, after much searching and poking, the RN managed to extract a sufficient quantity.

"We'll now send these samples to the GSK labs in Van Nuys, California," the nurse said, "and in three weeks or so, you'll come back for baseline blood work, and to get your meds."

"*Three* weeks?" I whined. "It takes that long?"

"Well," she responded, "as fast as one week, but I'd count on three if I were you."

"Ok," I said.

"You'll see the Doctor next," the nurse announced. "Why don't you grab something to eat in the meantime?"

"Do I have enough time to step outside for a smoke?" I asked.

"Sure," she replied, "but you'll have to go to the gas station across the freeway. There's no smoking anywhere on the hospital campus."

Odd, I thought, that hospital administrators deemed it safer to smoke at a facility specializing in the sale of volatile fuels than in a parking lot "on campus."

My step-dad and I returned from this ridiculous exercise (ridiculous inasmuch as I insisted on smoking), only to discover the doctor would not see me now. He and his wife had apparently just adopted two little girls, who were sick today.

My appointment with Dr. Borucki safely rescheduled for two days later, we hopped in the car and came back home, where I spent the remainder of the day dealing with stomach cramps and my newest malady, aching eyeballs.

So yesterday was a bad day, between a growing list of symptoms and a new delay in receiving treatment.

What am I to do now – poor pitiful me? Not really much of a choice, is there? I can either; (a) roll over and die; or (b) try to look at the bright side and move on.

Well, let's see… I'm surrounded by a loving family, including my parents, my brother and his fiancée; I've located a marvelous network of care-providers, only a few of which you've already met; and all my basic needs (food, shelter, clothing) are met with great care.

Oh yeah… and I am alive – meaning I still have a chance to work out that whole "legacy" thing.

Then you have to consider that all of us get to roll over and die eventually – so that rather takes the romance out of option "a."

What the hell, guess I'll keep my eye on the prize and move forward.

For many of us, however, simply deciding to move forward isn't enough to pull us out of the pit of despair. I recently met a young man who, completely healthy & symptom-free, found out after a routine blood test that he was HIV-positive. He suffered a deep depression that kept him from leaving his home for a year. His list of things to be thankful for just seemed too paltry when stacked against the list of reasons not to get out of bed.

My recommendation, had I known him then, would have been to dance.

Yes, I said *dance*.

There are actually psychological studies that show people's disposition follows their behavior. In other words, if you *act* happy, you have an edge up toward *being* happy. Try it in the privacy of your own room next time you're feeling down… just dance. Even if the very silliness of the exercise brings the slightest Mona Lisa smile to the corners of your lips, I've done my job.

"And he sang as he watched and waited 'til his billy boiled. Who'll come a-waltzing Matilda with me?"

Chapter 7: The Tenuous Relationship between Aid and AIDS

GREETINGS FROM GOD'S (BUSH'S) COUNTRY - East Texas (YIPPY KI YEY)!

My parents live in a dry county, which means we have to drive 30 miles to legally purchase a six-pack of beer. Fortunately, there's a loophole in the law that allows Christians in good standing to purchase alcoholic beverages from respectable, God-fearing restaurants. But there's a catch... (and I'm getting ahead of myself).

I've been craving a margarita... the lime, the salt on the rim, the cool yet warm sensation as the miraculous potion slithers down my throat, warming the spirit as it pleasantly numbs the mind. Inhibitions rapidly fade and I wake up hours later, curled up on the table – lost in my enjoyment of what's left of a crispy taco as an audience of onlookers applauds.

At least that was the experience I had hoped for when my step-dad graciously offered to take me to Casa Ole' last week. It seems that, in East Texas, IDs are not used as proof of age, however. While I'm clearly older than 21, the waitress informed me IDs were used here to keep tabs on local drinkers. My identity was to be sent electronically to a local law enforcement agency that apparently tracks public misconduct and improper treatment of various Mexican foods.

None of this was nearly as disturbing to me as the fact I'd left my wallet at home. Translation: no margaritas tonight.

I did learn one valuable lesson, however - which is that Mexican food is an entirely different animal when consumed with Dr. Pepper. I don't recommend it.

Idea for a Visa spot: "Tyler, Texas boasts some of the best Tex-Mex food this side of the Pecos. You can drink to your heart's content and eat 'til the cows come home, so bring your appetite, some cash, and your valid Texas ID card, because in Tyler, they don't take kindly to drinkers, and they don't take crap from outsiders: God -- He's everywhere you want to be."

I guess all I'm saying is that Dorothy was starting to realize she wasn't in Kansas anymore. This was East Texas. Things were different here....

And "things" were different in all sorts of other ways, too – as I discovered when I looked into getting health care.

Since our country has no federal guarantee of health care for its citizens (health care in the USA being a privilege and not a right), a huge number of local, county, and state organizations, both public and private, have sprung up to fill the many gaps. This has resulted in myriad location-specific procedures you must follow in order to receive aid, varying greatly from town to town, and sometimes within parts of towns, across the entire nation.

My case should make an excellent example for anyone whose need for assistance is as dire as mine, since I'm a recent transplant to Tyler, Texas, and was therefore completely ignorant of its various agencies, organizations and application procedures. Worst-case scenario – you're broke, you're disabled, and you're in a new town where you don't know anyone…. What aid is available and how do you go about applying for it?

When in Rome…

The next time I ventured to a Mexican restaurant in Tyler, I brought my ID card and got a margarita. Through trial and error, I had discovered how to get something I wanted. Unfortunately, applying for aid in the USA is a lot like that. But never despair – consider instead a thankful approach. In other words, be thankful that aid exists, and help is on the way. As long as you keep your cool and jump through the hoops, there are people out there who want to help. You just have to find them.

You will need a phone, a sense of humor, a phonebook, a sense of humor and a friend or family member to cart you around town. It will be helpful if you both agree ahead of time to remain cool and calm. Prepare to be shuffled from agency to agency, often ending up back where you started after finding out you were simply asking the wrong questions.

Each agency will tend to address only one or two issues. For example; Social Security Disability may cover living expenses, but can't offer you any medical assistance; a local free clinic may provide free medical care, but can't offer prescription assistance, and so on.

As you work your way around this network, you'll discover it creates a web of assistance that has no formal structure – as various organizations have sprung up to fill the gaps the federal government fails to address. One can only hope these gaps have been filled in your town in your time of need.

And try not to get frustrated with the various caseworkers and volunteers you'll come in contact with. Look at it this way – imagine you were a politician who helps to establish funding for a local organization to provide food and shelter for HIV and AIDS patients. Then imagine your constituents discovered there were several private organizations in place that already successfully addressed these needs. You'd lose your job! The moral: when someone tells you they can't help you, trust that there is someone else who can. It's a puzzle you've got to put together.

So we end up with this hodge-podge of scattered organizations, each with a very specific charter, each doing its part to help without squandering their very limited resources. Have pity on them – be patient with them – and even consider volunteering for them. By becoming involved, you can help assure no one falls through the cracks in our flawed web of assistance. Helping others also makes you feel better about yourself, and God knows we can all use a little of that medicine.

Here's a list of helpful organizations in Tyler, along with a brief description of their charters. While the list will be different in your town, I think you'll get the idea:

Social Security Administration (SSA): provides a monthly income for disabled persons. The screening process usually takes three to four months, and is based primarily on your doctor's recommendation. If approved, your disabled status may open other opportunities for aid, such as Medicaid, Medicare, and even supplementary security income (SSI). If you've lost your Social Security Card, apply for a new one; you're going to need it as you apply for assistance.

Local free clinic, or local free clinic for HIV and AIDS: This local clinic is my most important resource, since they provide me with primary health care free of charge. You will simply have to ask around to find similar resources in your town.

Local hospital emergency room: Don't forget this resource in times of need. You are guaranteed emergency room treatment even when you can't afford to pay for it. It saved my life once, and it could save yours.

Medicaid: In Tyler, Texas, Medicaid (indigent health services) is handled by the Texas Dept of Health and Human Services. Your eligibility for this program will be determined, in part, by the Social

Security Administration's decision regarding your disability status. In other words, they may tell you to call back after that determination is made. In my case, my disability income (assuming I get it) will be too high to qualify, which turns my attention to Medicare.

Medicare: In Tyler, Medicare (federal health benefits program primarily designed for retirees and the disabled) applications are handled through the Social Security Administration. I was infuriated when I was told that, assuming I even qualified, there would be a two-year wait before receiving any benefits. Then I realized that the local free clinic was already taking care of my medical needs – another example of how the network of services compliments, rather than duplicates, its assistance.

Other governmental resources: In Tyler, the office of Special Health Resources of Texas (SHRT) provides a safety net for many of the gaps left by the other programs. While their funding is extremely limited, these resources can be a godsend during that tenuous period after applying for other aid and before receiving it. SHRT paid for my prescriptions and gave me a $25 gift card for a local grocery chain, along with an offer to pay half our utilities for three months each year. I also got my name on a two-year waiting list for housing. While this may not sound like a lot of aid, it was a lot to me. Especially considering all the other assistance I'd found, I was starting to feel like a person again. Even in my condition, someone thought I was worth helping, and that felt pretty good.

Pharmaceutical research: If you live in a town that sports a university medical center, like Tyler, and especially if you are "drug naïve" (a medical term meaning "untreated") and willing to be a guinea pig, you might see if there are any studies you qualify for. You'll be helping to advance the science of AIDS treatment options and enjoy free meds at the same time. Additionally, most studies pay the subjects a modest amount for their trouble. I get $35 for each visit. While this may not sound like much, it's the most money I've had in my pocket since moving here.

Counseling: In Tyler, the Center for Well-Being offers a free weekly group session for HIV and AIDS patients. While I went the first time just to try to make some new friends, I must admit it felt great to vent to strangers! Amazing how a little screaming can soothe the soul.

Food Bank: I had to swallow some pride before visiting here, but was glad I did. Given the financial strain I've put on my parents, this turned out to be a real blessing. We received a generous box of truly good food (I'd estimate $80 or more in value) and were invited to come back every two weeks. That should help the budget at home a little. While I imagine this is rare, Tyler AIDS Services also offers some housing for those in need – the point being you should always ask what other services they offer. You may be surprised.

Parents Family and Friends of Lesbians and Gays (PFLAG): PFLAG is not an assistance program, though it is collectively one of the largest organizations in the world advocating fair treatment of gays and lesbians. I list it here as a networking opportunity that may be able to assist you in finding other local sources of aid. Just show up at the next meeting and introduce yourself. These are friendly people who could point you in the right direction.

The United Way Referral Line: call 211. This can be an excellent resource. I found the caseworkers to be very friendly, and they even followed up the following week to see how I was doing and suggest additional resources.

Free Clinics and other private resources: Check out local churches and private foundations and organizations. Your best resource is word of mouth. Only one thing is certain: if you don't ask for help, you won't find it.

Pharmaceutical companies: All the pharmaceutical spots I see on TV these days include a message at the end regarding those of us in need of help in buying our medications. Apparently prompted by fear of legislation that would put price caps on their profits, the pharmaceutical companies simultaneously adopted a "kinder, gentler" approach for indigent folk like myself. Don't get me wrong, either – in the absence of federal protection, I'll take any help I can get. In the case of pharmaceutical companies, however, this means you'll just have to examine each prescription and contact the companies individually. While there's no help for generics, I suspect the savings you'll enjoy by choosing generics, when possible, will far outweigh any reduced pricing offered by the brand-name companies. As an example, the emergency room doctor originally prescribed the brand-name drug Diflucan for my thrush. The prescription for 15 pills cost nearly $6 per pill. When the thrush came back, my new doctor prescribed Fluconazole, the generic version of Diflucan. The Fluconazole cost only $1 per pill. And make no mistake – pharmaceutical generics are chemically identical to their brand-name cousins, which should make for a no-brainer when it comes to choosing. Your doctor may have additional suggestions on how to minimize or eliminate your prescription expenses.

Metropolitan Community Church (MCC): This is the largest pro-human rights gay, lesbian and bisexual organization on the planet. Whether you are religious or not, whether you are gay or not, I guarantee you'll find a sense of community there, assuming you're lucky enough to live in a town where they meet. Unfortunately for me, there's no MCC in Tyler, so I've been attending services at Unity with my parents. Unity offers less traditional-style services, and I was welcomed with open arms -- the point being that attending the church of your choice can help you remain spiritually centered, offer a sense of community and provide you with both kinds of opportunities: getting help and helping others.

I hope this short list is helpful – if not in pointing you in the right direction, then at least in promoting the right attitude as you begin the arduous task of finding needles in haystacks. The needles are, after all, out there. You just have to trust in the network and be persistent in your quest.

Chapter 8: Instinct or Extinct: a few words on bias

TODAY IS MONDAY, JANUARY 16, 2006. It is Martin Luther King, Jr. day, a federal holiday – and I decided to take a little time to consider people like Dr. King who have collectively shouted from the highest places, "We have waited long enough.... Let us put an end to bias."

I believe that bias is dangerous at best – at its worst, it is genocide. Whether disguised in political frameworks or (more typically) blind religious faith as righteous and necessary, it remains dangerous and deadly.

Shortly after relocating to Tyler from Wilmington, North Carolina, I found many resources for aid and assistance, but was surprised when I tried to connect with the gay community. Try as I might, I couldn't find one! No meetings, no favorite coffee shops or restaurants; Tyler, Texas lends new meaning to the term "dry county," since its as hard to find the gay community as it is to locate a bottle of wine. The reason for Tyler's invisible gay community seems to boil down to one word: bias.

Shirley Chiesa is not originally from Tyler – like me, she's moved here from places far from Tyler's many lakes, rolling hills and deeply-rooted religiosity. When I met Shirley at her office at Tyler AIDS Services, we became instant friends. I was there to inquire about the food bank, and she was there to help. After I filled out a couple of simple forms, we had a chance to chat. Shirley told me about a personal experience that provided insight about local bias.

Shirley lectures at various schools and organizations on local issues surrounding HIV and AIDS. After a recent lecture to a civic group, Shirley was approached by a middle-aged woman who thanked her for the presentation, then smugly added, "… but you know dear, we don't have that problem in Tyler…." This self-assured woman was so comforted by her own bias, she hadn't heard a word of Shirley's presentation.

My brother's fiancée is an attorney for a local law firm. Recently a young attorney, fresh out of school, was interviewing for a position there. The formal part of the interview went well, after which the young man was asked the open-ended question that allowed him to dig his own grave: "Tell us about yourself."

The young man began by bragging about his parents – how wealthy, respected, successful and powerful they were – but quickly transitioned to more important matters, such as the "gay problem." He proudly announced to his interviewers that one of his first acts as a new homeowner was to join a neighborhood campaign to kick the gays out.

While Tyler supports an enormously warm and generous AIDS services network, it does so under the apparent condition that we don't talk about it. A community dressed in white picket fences, perfectly groomed lawns and freshly painted homes fails to provide a sense of community for gays, lesbians and bisexuals, the majority of whom remain closeted and fearful of standing out.

In its least malicious form, bias is simply the result of insufficient data. In its most common form, however, it is born of a conscious effort to ignore the facts because of a political agenda or religious dogma.

If part of the human experience is to suffer from personal biases, then another part must be to understand and eradicate them, since our biases make it hard for us to process important data from our environment and even from our own bodies.

Americans display a self-imposed cultural naiveté – a unique brand of ethnocentricity that is utterly unforgivable in the modern era of easy access to information. We cling to our absurd prejudices with religious fervor, screaming that blacks are inferior and God hates fags.

Six years ago, I bought a neighborhood tavern in Wilmington, NC and quickly set about to make it a live-blues venue. It wasn't long, however, before a patron approached me with a time-tested solution to what she called "the black problem." "You just make white memberships $10," she said, "and the blacks pay $100."

When I told her how offensive I found her suggestion, she simply threatened a boycott. The boycott lasted two months, and business suffered. No owner since the bar opened in the 1950s had allowed blacks inside, and the clientele was angry.

Every now and then, however, one of the tightly-knit "anti-black" crowd would stop by for a beer, and inevitably a few struck up conversations with black patrons. Gradually, the old crowd began to come back in pairs, then threesomes, and finally in full force of ten or fifteen people at a time. The boycott was stymied after some whites began to realize that blacks were not that different from them, after all. This miracle did not take place on a TV screen or because of a lecture or brochure. It happened because, after ignoring all the facts for decades, these folks were finally confronted with the "inferior race," and lo and behold, found that they were pretty nice people. Our simple grass roots approach had succeeded in educating those who had refused to learn otherwise. Imagine that.

A few weeks later, the recovering racists sent their gossip-hound to ask me privately, "Are you queer?"

"As a three-dollar bill," I replied.

From that moment on, we all got along famously: the faggots, the blacks, the Mexicans and the rednecks – all one big happy family.

Our Age of Information has proven appallingly ineffective in combating violence, partly because the hate groups also use technology and media to espouse their flawed agendas. The cure, therefore, for racial prejudice is to *meet* black people, and the cure for "God hates gays" is to *meet* gay people.

Unfortunately, in Tyler, there *are* no gay people – or rather, they are unseen, safely imperceptible so as not to cause wrinkles in the fabric of devout respect for The Creator.

I'm not one of those flamboyant transvestite types, but I respect those who are. I have never marched in a gay pride parade, but I deeply respect those who do. I'm just a conservative type you'd never guess in a million years was gay, but I'm honest at home and at work and *everywhere* about who I am – and that makes me "out" of the closet. I think of it as my own personal grass roots effort to educate people on the only level that matters: teaching by way of personal introduction – "Hey," the guy recounts later to friends, "I met a queer today and he seemed like a right nice fella."

That's why I find the lack of community among gay people in Tyler so disturbing, because we'll never be accepted until people meet us. By hiding, we only help to perpetuate the myths that "God hates gays" and "There is no AIDS problem here." These attitudes are beyond being offensive. They can kill.

If hanging on to our biases can kill, then we can take comfort in knowing that letting go of them can enhance our own lives. Here's a personal experience that illustrates my point:

I spent much of my time as a high school senior applying and testing for admission to the US Air Force Academy in Colorado. The testing involved physical abilities and, at one point, even an EEG (Electroencephalogram, or brain wave test). As I reclined in a comfortable chair, electrodes were attached to my forehead and I was asked to relax, but not sleep. The test involved studying my alpha waves, which occur when a subject is awake, but tranquil. In any case, they got no usable data from excessively agitated or sleeping subjects – which quickly became an issue.

I hadn't intended to create problems for the attendant nurse, but nonetheless had to be nudged awake several times during testing. He explained that my alpha waves had transitioned to theta waves, which signals the first stage of sleep.

The first couple of times he woke me, I thought it was a coincidence, but by the seventh and eighth wakings, I had discovered a relationship between my experience and the printouts that indicated "theta," or "sleeping." The relationship was pictures!

Each time he nudged me awake, the blackness on the inside of my eyelids had just begun to morph into basic shapes (like lines, circles and squares) and colors. The relationship was so profound and exact that I began to wonder whether visualizing such shapes might help to induce sleep – a trick that would be handy on those nights when I found sleep elusive.

So I tried it, and it worked! Night after night, those shapes provided my last conscious thoughts. As with dreams, I sometimes had complete control over the shapes and colors and sometimes no control. They were always in motion and ultimately morphed into various stages of detail – the beginnings, I presume, of a dream, though I could never recall anything after the first few seconds or minutes. This is a technique I still use to get to sleep, and I adopted it only because I was paying attention. I wasn't blinded by a personal bias that might have instructed me to just take a sleeping pill. Experts developed sleeping pills, but my technique was developed by paying attention… and keeping an open mind.

I'm still about two weeks out from beginning treatment for the AIDS virus, though my health seems to have improved dramatically over the weekend. As late as Friday, during my visit with Dr. Borucki, I was hobbling and doubled over with abdominal cramps. I was miserable!

The doc seems to have found a pharmaceutical regimen that has tackled almost all my symptoms. My current drug lineup includes:

Sulfamethoxazole, a cross-spectrum antibiotic to attack various infections my low CD-4 count can't handle

Fluconazole, to treat yeast infections (thrush) and generally prescribed as a preventative measure for many patients with a CD-4 count under 200

Nexium, a drug that has virtually cured the painful abdominal cramping caused by the fluconazole

Nystatin and Triamcinolone Acetone Cream, an excellent topical ointment that has already begun to make dramatic improvements in my skin, and finally:

Trazodone, an ineffective anti-depressant, now commonly prescribed as a mild aid for sleep (yeah, even the sleeping-technique guru needs a little help these days).

So my night sweats have subsided, I'm getting restful sleep, I feel generally good and my skin is clearing up. You might say my reasons-to-get-out-of-bed list just got a little longer and my woe-is-me list a little shorter.

Today is Martin Luther King, Jr. Day. Today is a good day.

Chapter 9: Coping

August, die she must,

The autumn winds blow chilly and cold;

September I'll remember

A love once new has now grown old.

  -- Simon and Garfunkel

TODAY IS WEDNESDAY, JANUARY 18, 2006. I normally get up about 4:00 a.m., but yesterday I woke six hours late, feeling exhausted. After two days of feeling well, I had a headache and fever and felt nauseated. Yesterday I stayed in my bathrobe and missed my weekly support group session, which would have been my second visit there.

Yesterday a cold front blew through Tyler. I was sitting on the back porch, watching the trees bending slightly against the gentle breeze, when one of these gusts brought with it a twenty-degree drop in temperature. And just like that, I remembered I have AIDS.

This happens from time to time. I'll be daydreaming or making plans or watching a movie – my attention turned completely toward topics outside myself – when, carried on a frigid gust, comes a gentle reminder, and I remember: "Oh yeah, I'm dying... Time is short... Don't make too many plans...."

But growing old also comes at a cost. I just received a warm letter from my grandmother, whose disposition has always inspired me. "Have made friends here," she wrote. "Would you believe some of the help are great grandchildren of my old friends – who are all gone.... I too think a lot of Phyllis, Dane and Bobby and all my brothers and sisters who are gone. Why am I still here? They all had so much to give. I feel so useless. Like you said, there must be a reason.... My motto is 'keep smiling.'"

My grandmother turns 102 this year, and I think it's largely due to her "keep smiling" credo. Still, I wonder what it would be like to outlive so many of one's family and friends. She has lost children, has no surviving brothers, sisters or friends – no peers. She can no longer enjoy laughter with an old friend over an "inside joke," because there are no more inside jokes. She is an anachronism, a fine butter churn in an era when butter churns are no longer used – a lone weathered tree on a vast grassy plain, which she alone can recall was once a forest of saplings.

Last night the sky was unusually clear, and I couldn't help but smile at the sight of Orion. For as long as I can remember, Orion has provided my first view upon looking at the night sky. I can't explain why, but when I look upwards, Orion is always the center of my field of view. As a child, I allowed myself to imagine this ancient warrior was watching over me – a superstitious viewpoint I hold even now. Aside from the tremendous odds against my always "knowing" where to look, I find an intriguing kind of comfort in the thought that the stars will always be there, even if I won't be.

But that's not entirely true, is it? The stars of Orion are, after all, in motion. Every year, the constellation changes ever so slightly, and over millennia will someday not be recognizable. And one by one, these stars will burn out…. Someday, Orion, too, will die.

It would probably be unhealthy to invest too much energy into such melancholy reflection. Still, it's healthy to recall, from time to time, that there is no such thing as "permanent."

I love a good paradox. If you pay attention, you'll discover that life is full of them.

Paradoxical that I finally feel free of the more mundane obligations that have eaten up my life until now. In a very real sense, I no longer feel bound in *time*.

You've heard the expression, "it won't be the end of the world" if you don't get something done. Now that it *is* the end of the world, nothing needs to be done, and I am finally freed to pursue things that truly interest me. The cost of that freedom is suffering and death.

Isn't it odd that we don't really appreciate our lives until they are at an end?

But what an honor has been my life!... to exist!... to love!... How fortunate am I to have discovered so many things – incredible things – wondrous things, like Yellowstone and music and Mexican food and people who love me no matter what? And even pain... *especially* pain... I'm thankful for that, too, because it is the sole condition for proving I exist – I feel pain, therefore I am.

I *am*. Even knowing I will not always *be*, I *am* -- and that is enough. "When the child was a child," says the angel in Wim Wenders' classic film *Wings of Desire*, "he laughed in playgrounds and cried when he skinned his knee." Without darkness, light would have no value or meaning. Without death, there would be no life. If I've been granted a seat in a game, who am I to complain when it is someone else's turn to play?

Coping.... The word suggests I'm dealing with a difficult issue, but today it doesn't seem hard to wrap my mind around it – I don't feel like I'm *coping*, which, I suppose, is an indicator that I'm coping pretty well (at least today). When I was an Air Force cadet, my squadron commander gave some advice that's held me in good stead. We had just won the Squadron of the Year award, an accomplishment marked by a formal banquet. "The secret to success," he said during his acceptance speech, "is making it look easy, even when its not."

It was a curious thing to say, but it got me thinking.

I was an average student at the Air Force Academy, graduating with a 2.5 grade-point-average, placing me squarely in the middle of the curve. This mediocre performance was the result of a wide range of grades, however: A's in English, B's in engineering and philosophy and C's in science. I only failed one class – statistics. I hated statistics because it was boring and impossibly difficult. To make matters worse, the failure put me on academic probation and meant I'd have to sit through the class a second time.

Retaking statistics was to prove entirely different from *taking* it, however, as I tried to apply the lesson learned from my squadron commander: "The secret to success is making it *look* easy, even when its not." As the instructor began each day, I simply told myself, "This is easy."

And it was!

I found myself mesmerized by the rationale behind statistics, fascinated by the math. Each day after class, I'd rush back to my room to complete the homework. Statistics wasn't impossible, after all – it was, in fact *easy!* I had discovered, for my own personal use, the tenet that by making something *look* easy, it necessarily *becomes* easy. From failing statistics the previous semester, I succeeded the second go-'round with a remarkable 100 percent average, earning the only A+ you will find on my transcript. This became one of the most powerful lessons I had ever stumbled across, and it literally changed my life.

And you can see that lesson operating in history. In 1880 a French company began building a canal across a 50-mile stretch of land in a country that was to become Panama. Soon, however, the workers began to die – a few at first, but then by the thousands. The more men they sent in, the more died. Eventually, France gave up on the project, calling it an "impossible folly."

In 1899, the United States took over the project. One hundred years later, the same locks provide passage through the thriving industrial miracle that shaves 1800 miles off a trip from Boston to San Francisco. How did the United States succeed where France failed? How do you make possible the impossible?

You simply make it look easy.

Before attempting excavation, the United States sent in doctors, who discovered the malaria that killed so many French workers was carried by the many mosquitoes in the area. The mosquitoes thrived in the stagnant marshes and cesspools of the cities and villages. So Step One was an all-out campaign against an insect. Marshes were drained, and Panama received the gift of indoor plumbing and a sewer system. The rest, as they say, is history. When the Americans made a daunting task look easy, it *became* easy, or at least easier.

The corollary to our tenet seems to involve fear. The French were stopped in their tracks not by mosquitoes and malaria, but by their fear of them. Their fear of failure bred the failure they found. This revelation is profoundly instructional, since it brings us to a startling conclusion: that the task itself is not difficult – it is our fear of the task that makes life seem hard.

Time after time, I've discovered the "daunting" task is made impossible only when we fear it… never when we resolve to "make it look easy."

Part of our collective human experience involves the nagging question of what tomorrow may bring. There is no way of knowing ahead of time. "The best laid plans of mice and men often go awry," Robert Burns famously said.[3] I may gradually waste away and be gone in five, ten or twenty years, or, like my grandmother, live to 102. My illness has changed my outlook a bit, that's all.

My fear of death, much like my childhood fear of broccoli, turns out to be based on the faulty premise that the experience might be unpleasant. "Hey," I announce, through ravenous bites, "pass the cheese. This isn't so bad, after all."

Dear Grandma,

Thank you for the heartfelt letter. You write poetically and are always a joy to me. I'm enclosing the latest chapter of my book – a chapter inspired by your letter. I hope you like it.

I've been feeling good. Just got a call today and the doctor says the test results came in early, so I get to start medication on Wednesday instead of waiting another week, like we were planning. He says I'll actually get worse for a week or two after starting medication, as my body adjusts, but should improve dramatically after that.

---

[3] Burns put it this way: "The best laid schemes o' mice an' men / Gang aft a-gley."

It's been unseasonably warm here, but I'm not complaining. I slept with the window open last night. The breeze smelled like freshly-washed linen – felt so comforting on my skin. I wish every night was like that! Reminded me of taking a nap on grandpa's bed in the summertime when I was very small, indeed.

Can't wait to see you in April, and am looking forward to your next letter.

P.S. – Don't you believe for a second that you are useless. Your wisdom continues to inspire everyone whose lives you touch. I, for one would be lost without you.

Chapter 10: White Noise

It's good to shut up sometimes.

-- Marcel Marceau

MY PARENTS LIVE IN A NEW CONDOMINIUM. Behind it is a small porch, where I sit to smoke. My view includes a thin strip of lawn enclosed by a wooden privacy fence. Above the fence, a small wood towers against the early morning sky – the leafless winter silhouettes providing stark contrast to the bright glow of the city beyond. The woods are enclosed by a highway, the hum of engines and tires on pavement ever-present. But not today. Two-thirty on a Sunday morning, and the world is still -- the silence of a misty rainfall betrayed only by a rhythmic dripping in the drainpipe. Like a distant tribal drum beat, this reverberation transforms the scene, the fence becomes a stockade – the trees a primeval forest....

I've always been fascinated by environmental sounds – within which I imagine music inspired by the various frequencies I hear. Like the continuous chords of the bagpipe, this background "music" can inspire the careful listener with endless possibilities for new melodic compositions, which I invariably end up quietly humming to myself. Occasionally, I stumble across a melody that I think is pretty catchy, though it is invariably lost in the clutter of daily distractions.

My first memory of melodies imbedded in noise is as a child, riding in the back seat of the family's 1968 Pontiac. I heard in the purr of the engine several continuous notes that made an accidental chord. I began humming to myself -- starting with the dominant frequency, but quickly branching out into an original melody, the gist of which has been long forgotten. This practice was also an amusing pastime years later, as a young Air Force navigator, when I discovered the drone of four turboprop engines provided musical cues. These included strong dominant tones; a rhythmic beat caused by the four engines' waveforms being slightly out of synch; and the sheer volume, meaning I no longer had to hum my compositions quietly. Now, I could belt them out like an opera star, and no one would ever know.

Finding order within chaos seems to be a universal experience, as when we see shapes in clouds; or find music within the white noise of the rain or even an aircraft engine. It seems to be a uniquely human activity, requiring little if any conscious effort. It even seems to require the absence of conscious effort. The only requirement is stillness – stillness of the mind and of the body. In other words, "It's good to shut up sometimes."

A couple of days ago I was sitting on the back porch, missing the friends I left behind in North Carolina, listening to the gusty wind blowing through the treetops. I closed my eyes and realized this sound was indistinguishable from the crash of ocean waves on the beach. Suddenly, I was back in North Carolina, my friends nearby – all this personal comfort found within the static of the wind.

"White noise" is defined as all audible frequencies performed at equal volumes – creating the familiar "radio static" sound. If this sound contains all audible frequencies, does it not make sense that we may find within it the sounds we seek? And if white noise contains all the notes and all the music ever written, why is it so hard for us to accept that the blur of our hectic lives contains all the keys to our way through our most pressing problems? Without any effort, our stillness allows the hidden powers within our own minds to project the answers within us onto a canvas containing all the answers.

The clutter of daily habit keeps us from creative solutions – which sometimes require that we stop trying so hard. Just sit back and relax. The reply will come if you simply listen to the white noise. We sometimes find it difficult to sleep, because going to bed is the first time in the day we're still, and all the creative solutions of the day come flooding into our minds – a good argument for maintaining a bedside notepad.

My notepad now includes a wish list of personal milestones I would like to achieve before I die. Once I collected a few wishes, I began to prioritize them, and was surprised to realize my greatest wish was out of my hands: the forgiveness of my family and friends.

As undeserving as I am, I wish to be forgiven for living most of my life completely self-absorbed, rarely taking time from my busy life to give to you, sometimes when you needed me most. Now that its too late, I finally see how trivial my problems were, and I miss all the wasted opportunities forever lost… opportunities to know you better… opportunities to tell you how much you mean to me…opportunities to thank God for the day you were born. I was lost in the static.

You may be angry with me for other reasons, such as bringing into your life the tragedy of my circumstances. I want you to know that I wouldn't leave you behind if I had a choice. I regret leaving all of you behind. Forgive me.

My wish for you is peace – that you may rest easily each night in the comforting warmth of understanding how much your friendship has meant to me – that no one deserves to be regretful, and least of all someone whose gentle spirit has touched and enhanced so many lives as yours. Rest gently… I wish that for you.

And if I am so fortunate as to be loved as much as you are loved, I hope my passing will be celebrated, not mourned. This is my greatest wish, since there is nothing bigger in heaven or earth than to love and be loved. The rest is nonsense.

Some of the friends from my former (undiagnosed) life have stayed in touch, while others remain silent – declining to answer my letters or phone messages. Just as it's easier to ignore a message about starving children in Africa, some people can't bring themselves to deal with the sad realities of other peoples' misfortune. Momentarily hurt and dismayed by these vanishing friendships, I decided not to take their silence personally. Their failure to respond is a result of their own inability to cope with any crisis, especially those involving other people.

In the calm of the early morning mist I found the tranquility of forgiveness and understanding – remembering that my role in all this is far easier than the roles of my family and friends. I have become the burden, and they the gentle souls who sustain me. How can I find fault in those who simply find the load too cumbersome? And how thankful am I for those who have stood by my side!

Were our roles reversed, wouldn't I want to take a loved one's illness from them – wouldn't I want to offer myself up to the gods if it would save them? Rather than mope over my fair weather friends, shouldn't I, then, be thankful for those whose love sustains me still? Shouldn't I be thankful that I'm the one who's sick, not them? My wish has been granted. All is well in my world.

Tomorrow I begin my medication – my treatment for a fatal and incurable disease. I am to be a subject in a noble experiment designed to make a difference in the lives of others stricken with AIDS. I can handle all of this only because I know a secret: I am practiced in the fine art of finding shapes in the clouds and music in the rain -- I know how to be still.

Chapter 11: Prophets and Healers

I GREW UP IN DODGE CITY, KANSAS (yes, Viginia, there is a Dodge City). In spite of its one-time importance as a market and train depot – the end of the line for the once-vital cattle drives from Texas on their way by train to Kansas City – Dodge City remains a small town in the midwestern part of the state. This is a good thing, because it has allowed the town to retain some of its Old-West ambiance. Even today, "Howdy" is the greeting as you pass strangers on the street. It's not uncommon to see locals in cowboy hats, and Western boots still accessorize a gentleman's formal attire. You can't visit Dodge City without stopping by Boot Hill – the quintessential Old-West tourist complex, named for those said to have been buried after gunfights with their boots on. Boot Hill includes a faithful reproduction of Front Street, replete with museums, historical artifacts and the famous Long Branch Saloon, where they still serve real Sarsaparilla. With a little imagination, Boot Hill is a place where you can step directly from the twenty-first century to the rough-and-tumble nineteenth.

Within the museum collections at Boot Hill, visitors will find a small area dedicated to the proud heritage of a purveyor of fine elixirs – the snake oil salesman. These fearless souls wandered the frontier with a stock of miraculous medicines that promised to cure everything from malaria to decrepitude; from gout to influenza; from baldness to consumption and a mysterious illness known as "dropsy." The healing powers of the salesman's wares were, in fact, eclipsed only by the audacity of his showmanship. Formerly available exclusively to the crowned heads of Europe, these cures were now provided to the common man for the first time in history. Made with rare Artesian waters and kissed by herbs and spices so uncommon that not even botanists had heard of them, the "medicine" was absolutely guaranteed to fix whatever might be broke, your investment cheerfully refunded should it fail.

But alas, momma's gout only got worse, and the stuff made the dog sick, too. This is why the snake oil salesman had typically left town by first light, carefully routing his journey so as never to land in the same place twice. Like a tumbling tumbleweed, he led a solitary life, comforted only by the cash he collected along the way.

About a hundred years after the last traveling medicine man was buried in the real Boot Hill, I met one of his occupational descendants, a spiritual healer recommended to me by an acquaintance. I'm pretty level-headed when it comes to claims made by spiritual healers, but even the medical community is beginning to take stock in holistic medicine, including positive thinking, mind-over-body, and spiritual healing.

And, at that point, I could have used some healing. The doctor had warned me that the meds would make me feel worse for a while, and they did. After taking the melon-size capsules and pills, I experienced a complete loss of energy and severe abdominal cramping. So, my attitude toward the healer was, "What have I got to lose? If this guy was interested in curing me, why not give him a chance?"

In spite of my attempted open-mindedness, however, there was something about our exchange that made me uncomfortable.

From the start, it was clear that his fees were beyond my budget. He forecast that my treatment would require three visits and would not be effective unless I also began taking expensive herbal supplements that I would need to purchase through him.

He was very nice and sincere, however, so I let him down gently, explaining that my doctor had expressly forbidden the use of exotic supplements as potentially damaging to the effectiveness of my prescribed medications. When I hung up the phone, I imagined that was the end of that....

It wasn't.

Correctly assuming I'd been put off by the dollar figure, he called back a few days later, offering to perform the procedures (minus the herbal supplements) for the reduced price of a hug. He went on to say it would help him as well, because he was new in the business, and was required to conduct twenty-five healings before he could get into a professional psychic healers association.

I had already decided against psychic healing, but he seemed so sincere. When he insisted I allow him to come over and meet me in person, I simply couldn't bring myself to refuse. Mom nearly had a cow when she found out I had invited him over.

I was just trying to be nice – a personality flaw that has spawned a herd of cattle over the years.

"He's very friendly," I assured Mom after ending the call. "This'll just take a few minutes and I'll explain nicely that I'm not interested. He just wants to meet me."

The healer arrived a few minutes later, dressed in his work clothes, and asked if we had a private place to chat. I led him to the spare room, and he seemed slightly perturbed when mom joined us – though you couldn't have dragged mom away with a team of mules.

"I think we should start by discussing the nature of AIDS," he began, as we listened attentively.

"AIDS is actually transmitted inside nematodes that live in the bloodstream…."

"Hmmm, really?" I said as I glanced at mom, wondering if he might also be able to treat her for shock.

"These nematodes lay their larvae in your bloodstream, and this is how AIDS grows in you."

"You're speaking metaphorically, right?" Mom asked politely.

"No," the healer responded gravely.

He went on to explain how, by utilizing the latest "psychic frequency technology," he would attack these nematodes and their larvae on an atomic level, literally causing their valence electrons to spin clockwise, rather than counterclockwise.

After explaining all the aspects of his work, he felt compelled to tell us more about himself. "I'd rather you heard it from me," he added.

He went into some detail about his three-year stint in prison. I had heard enough. I was tired of all of it and began to gear up for his departure.

He wasn't finished with his pitch, however.

"I'd also like you to consider becoming a healer yourself," he began. "For $150, I can teach psychic frequency technology to you – which can be a lucrative business."

"Hmmm," I offered, as I escorted him to the door, "let me think about that...."

And that was, hopefully, the last time I'll have to deal with the psychic healer cum snake oil salesman.

I'm still not against trying psychic healing. I've heard too many success stories to ignore the phenomenon -- but I won't be buying the service from a phony, and I won't go against my doctor's advice, either. I've waited too long and worked too hard to get started on medical treatment to be so cavalier with my own survival.

Still, I found in the snake oil a most unexpected and unadvertised healing property. On the same day I began treatment for AIDS, I was also blessed with one of the most curative substances known to man – a good, healthy, heartfelt laugh.

Chapter 12: The Odyssey

ON JANUARY 28, 2006, I woke up at 5:30 and went out to sit on the porch while I waited for the coffee to brew. The cool, gusty breeze carried with it the scent of much-needed rain. My two nieces, whom I hadn't seen in years, were driving in from Dallas, which gave me something to look forward to, but the pre-dawn hours provided my quiet time… a time to reflect.

My doctor had warned me that, when I started the HIV regimen of medication, my health would likely decline before it started improving, but I don't think he anticipated the extent to which it was about to decline.

In December of 2005, I had been diagnosed with a CD-4 (or T-cell) count of 94, which planted me firmly in the category of "full-blown AIDS." With a viral load of over a million, I was in trouble. By the time I began treatment in January, my CD-4 count had dropped to seven, meaning the virus had almost completely destroyed my immune system.

My night sweats had become unbearable. I was running a 104-degree temperature nightly…waking every hour or so and going through five to eight sets of sweat-soaked pajamas each night. By morning, my pillow was wet enough to wring. During waking hours, constant headache and nausea provided proof that I was still alive. I suffered short-term memory loss and was frequently confused or disoriented.

My night-time fevers crept into my waking hours, cycling to 102 and frequently to 104 degrees, despite my consumption of gallons of ice water. More and more frequently, I would vomit up water after drinking too much.

On Jan. 26, my step dad took me to the hospital for an emergency visit with Dr. Borucki. My fever was spiking at 105 degrees and seemed unresponsive to our attempts to reduce it. Inside the maze of hospital corridors, I quickly became disoriented. No one seemed to know where Dr. Borucki's office was, and I found myself wandering from floor to floor, being sent down endless corridors. It required every ounce of composure I could muster not to break down in tears as a kindly hospital employee finally delivered me to the right department.

My fever, by then, had dropped to 102, but the doctor thought I should be hospitalized as a precaution. He said I had come down with pneumonia. After a little pleading, however, he agreed to let me return home, with strict instructions on managing my fever.

This is how I lived those first few weeks after beginning medication: feverish, confused, my head pounding, my stomach inside out. I felt near death, which seemed comforting, since it represented an end to the endless discomfort.

On February 7, I slipped into insanity. Dr. Borucki had advised me of the side effects of various drugs, including the curious experience of hallucinatory waking dreams. While I'm thankful for the heads up, no warning could have prepared me for losing my mind, nor will any attempt on my part to describe the experience adequately portray it.

It is not uncommon to experience hallucinations for a few days when starting AIDS medications. My hallucinations began while I was still sleeping. I remember taking time to readjust my perception on waking – saying to myself, "That was just a dream. I'm awake now. This is reality." The dream had seemed very real, however. The voices of various characters from my dream still reverberated in my room, as if the words had just been spoken.

I took a full ten minutes to wake – turned the television on and then off – decided to close my eyes for a moment and… voices booming! For an instant, I was in a crowded room with people, mostly men, I should have known but didn't. They were conducting business – some sort of meeting – and they were speaking loudly about me, rather than to me. Startled, I instantly opened my eyes and the voices stopped.

I got up and went to the toilet, trying to shake it off – stayed up another 15 minutes trying to convince myself that none of it had been real. My weariness conflicted with my fear the voices would return.

But I was weary. I wanted to sleep. So I lay back and closed my eyes again. The exact instant my eyes were closed, I sensed that I was somewhere in Europe – I heard a streetcar outside, and a kindly woman's voice talking about her garden. There was a loud knock at the door and the woman bade a visitor enter.

I bolted upright in bed, my eyes wide with fear. Which reality, I wondered, was real? Am I living a parallel life that intrudes the instant my eyes are closed? Who am I, really? What is wrong with me?

At that time, it seemed strangely logical to me that my current "reality" was rapidly slipping away, being usurped by the many existences that presented each time my eyelids closed for longer than a blink.

I began to believe that I had tapped into a very real list of alternate realities – a high-voltage connection to different places and experiences with a singular commonality – that they were all more real and more immediate than the reality I had always taken for granted. They were all more real than my own waking life.

I mentioned to my family that I was experiencing hallucinations, but there was no way to describe to them the sensation that they themselves seemed more and more like a dream to me.

Closing my eyelids transported me to an endless list of alternate dimensions, each threatening to obliterate all traces of my former world. I had the sensation of being drawn deeper, as if by gravity; I was falling into other worlds. This was unsettling at first, and became more frightening with each waking dream.

At length, I forced myself to shower and eat breakfast, fighting my fatigue and trying to stay awake at least a few hours.

On Thursday, my fever shot out of control and I was admitted to the University of Texas Hospital for pneumonia. Most memorable was the trip to the hospital – in my pajamas, my head out the window in the frigid winter air as I sprayed my face with water from a plastic bottle. All our prior efforts, including an agonizing bathtub full of ice, had failed to bring my temperature under 105 degrees. My main concern was to prevent my brain from cooking, but I was growing weary of the fight.

I was released the following Tuesday. My fever was stabilized. I had been diagnosed with a form of tuberculosis called micobacterium avium complex, or MAC – which turned out to be one of those illnesses for which the cure is nearly as bad as the disease. The pills caused ruthless nausea and a severe skewing of taste sensations – rendering most food inedible.

One afternoon in late February, I succumbed again to fever and headache, and lay back for a nap. I'm not sure how long I'd been out when I woke to the sound of shattering glass. Someone had broken into the house, and I could discern the voices of two intruders. My eyes, by now, were wide open as I stared at the open door to my bedroom and listened to their whispers.

"HELP!," I screamed – but to my horror, no sound came out. I was paralyzed! I could hear them coming down the hall, but I couldn't move. Staring at my own useless feet, I made a supreme effort, but could only manage the slightest movement of my toes – an almost imperceptible movement. "HELP ME," I tried to yell again, to no avail. My heart was racing as my fear turned to utter terror. At any instant, I knew, my assailant would appear in the doorway and find me utterly helpless. With every ounce of effort I managed, "mmmmma…" I was weeping and trying to say "mama." The sound of approaching footsteps proved that all was lost. In my desperation, I had betrayed my location. My assailant had found me.

But there was no assailant. The figure that appeared in my doorway was my mother. The simple sight of her broke the spell and I was no longer paralyzed. She sat beside me as I sobbed. "What's wrong with me?," I finally managed.

The next day I found myself once again unable to move – eyes wide open, my mind still switched into "sleep paralysis" mode, which is a mechanism ostensibly designed to keep us from acting out our dreams. But I wasn't sleeping, as my sense of dread grew to a crescendo. Suddenly my ankles were gripped by the powerful, icy hands of a being which began climbing up my legs – dragging its heavy, damp body over me as it climbed. I was frozen with fear – unable even to tilt my head down to see as the wriggling evil thing secured its purchase – its weight nearly crushing me as it progressed over my torso. Finally, I broke free from the spell and slid safely off the bed.

I was unable to sleep in my bed that night, fearful that the dream might recur. Like a child, I slept instead in my mom's bed, reassured that she would be near enough to wake me should the demons return.

The hallucinations and night terrors lasted only a couple of days, and as February gave way to March the mental fog began to clear, though I feared that my ability to think clearly had been permanently diminished.

So I stopped writing, and drifted into a sort of depression – a wait-and-see kind of depression – over the following few months as Dr. Borucki went about tackling symptoms, treating my fever, nausea and headaches.

By the end of May I went off the MAC medication, and my sense of taste returned to normal. My weight was still hovering, however, at an emaciated 140 pounds, a full 25 pounds below normal and 35 pounds below Dr Borucki's goal for me of 175.

Just as my illness had taken three years to develop to the point where I could no longer function independently, so my recovery was not about to be either quick or easy. As my immune system began the arduous task of "waking up," my body became more and more aware how sick it had become. I had been anesthetized against the pain of dying, and the price of survival was to begin the process of feeling all the pains and confusion of illness after illness.

I existed in a fog, unable to write, and spent my days and nights in bed.

Chapter 13: Beyond the Chapel Wall

ON THURSDAY, MARCH 16, 2006, I woke at 5:30 and waited for the coffee to brew while sitting on the back porch. My gaze penetrated the treetops and the haze of time, and I was transported twenty-five years back into my own personal age of innocence. In that world, I am a cadet at the United States Air Force Academy (USAFA). My physical tremors and mental fog give way to the steady hands and sharp mind of my former self. My weakness vanishes -- I am strong... unassailable... an all-American boy. The future's so bright, I gotta wear shades.

This is the story of how I made a movie at the US Air Force Academy. But to tell the story, I'm going to have to start with the debate team. The academy made debate seem like a good outlet. Debate made humor seem like a good outlet. And humor made film seem like a good idea – but I'm getting ahead of myself....

After struggling for two years to cope with military life and extreme time management, I found myself during the fall semester of 1982 fairly brimming with optimism. I was on the Dean's List, the Commandant's List and the Superintendent's List. I was student leader of the academy's debate team, and had just performed as master of ceremonies for a gala event celebrating the 35th anniversary of the United States Air Force, which was held downtown, in Colorado Springs.

Debate was fun, in a way, because I got to travel around the country, which meant I got to get away from the academy on weekends. Debate was still a high-stress, type-A personality competition, however, and I was only mediocre at it.

While I was somewhat enjoying the semi-liberty of traveling as a USAFA debater, I noticed that some cadets and students were having even more fun in what amounted to a stand-up comedy competition. I liked debate, but I *loved* making people laugh, so I made the transition in my junior year from the nail-biting formality of debate to the world of "After Dinner Speaking," which was a contest of who could write and deliver the funniest speech.

One day toward the beginning of my junior year, a group of my friends from the USAFA speech/debate team were sitting in my dorm room, talking about things that made us laugh. We had plenty of material, because the Academy was a very funny place. It wasn't uncommon, for example, to return to our rooms after class and find our underwear strewn about the room -- with a note from an Air Force major taped to the mirror: "Underwear should be folded in six-inch squares, not seven-inch squares." Now consider that this esteemed Air Force major was actually paid to monitor underwear folding – it was his job. That's pretty funny, if you think about it.

Laughing at the absurdity of our own predicament (even though the joke was on us) provided a way for us to cope. Levity cancels out oppression, at least for a minute. Then, in the midst of our laughter, someone said, "Guys, this is really good stuff. We should make a movie."

But then, someone *always* ends up saying that, with no intention of making a movie. But as we went back to our hectic daily schedules, I began working out the details of how a cadet might go about actually making a movie at the Air Force Academy. Not just any movie, either, but a bitingly sarcastic, positively subversive satire on cadet life. Underwear will now be folded into the shapes of animal crackers. That was a project I could sink my teeth into. "Beyond the Chapel Wall" was born.

Starting with notes from our brainstorming session, the film began to take shape in my mind. There was equipment to buy, a crew to assemble, a script to write and, oh yeah… I needed to learn the mechanics of filmmaking.

So I enrolled in Captain Rod Korba's filmmaking class, and set about organizing a fundraising scheme to purchase the camera and film I'd need. I came up with an idea to organize sales representatives in each of the Academy's forty squadrons to pre-sell t-shirts. We had three designs to choose from: one looked like a cadet uniform, Air Force blues, like those t-shirts that resemble tuxes. This one turned out to be a bad idea, since it had the dubious distinction of being both the most expensive to screen-print and the least popular of all the designs.

Another design featured an ominously oblique view of the cadet chapel, advertising "Beyond the Chapel Wall, coming soon to a theater near you."

The third design was the most popular, making up 90 percent of all the shirts we sold. It looked like a fraternity t-shirt, which was already humorous to us because fraternities have always been strictly banned at the service academies. Our fictional fraternity t-shirts showed "Sigma Phi Usafa," displaying the appropriate Greek symbols above "Sigma" and "Phi." Above our fictitious Greek word "Usafa," (pronounced "you-sah'-fah" for United States Air Force Academy) was a screw… as in "we were screwed."

The design struck a chord among the cadets and quickly produced nearly two thousand dollars, most of which was earmarked for film stock.

The objective of Captain Korba's filmmaking class was, not surprisingly, to make a film. Each of the fifteen or so students in the class was to submit a script, and the captain would choose one as our class project. My submission was a short tale about a cadet who used humor to help his classmates cope with life at the Academy. It wasn't, in my opinion, a very good script, but it benefited from the fact that I was apparently the only student taking the class for reasons other than an easy "A" – my way of saying the other scripts were even less promising than mine.

The academic environment at the Academy is protected by a policy of academic freedom, which promotes free thinking with the promise of a no-retribution clause. Officially, in a classroom environment, both faculty and students are allowed to say and think whatever they think (even remarks betraying our mistrust of the powers that be, for example) without fearing penalty. What's said in class stays in class.

I make the point only because it turned out to be untrue. Before the class had a chance to shoot the first frame of film, one of my classmates shared the script with his commanding officer, who, in turn shared it with the Commandant of Cadets – a brigadier general, no less. The humorless general didn't like the plot and demanded we remove all the jokes. That way, he reasoned, we might be able to use the class project as a recruitment film.

We were crestfallen. Our 10-page script was censored down to a paragraph. The general's "recruitment" film never came together and we spent the remainder of the semester reading about filmmaking, rather than making films ourselves. I did learn some valuable lessons in the class however, such as editing techniques, camera angles, and the sanctity and power of the script: never, ever let the script out of your hands.

By the winter semester of my senior year, we were ready to begin shooting. Unlike the failed attempt at a short film the previous semester, the script for "Beyond the Chapel Wall" was scathingly satirical. There were only three copies of the script, and they were used on a top-secret, need-to-know basis – returned to the safety of my personal possession each day after shooting wrapped.

My motto was: "It's easier to make apologies than get permission." In later years, Nike would simplify the same sentiment into their famous slogan, "Just do it." The script had been written with the idea of using all the locations of cadet legend and lore: the forbidden secret tunnel system, the cadet chapel, Bennigan's (a favorite hangout), and dorm-room and classroom scenes. On one occasion, we were busted using empty beer bottles as movie props, and I was given demerits, restrictions (loss of weekend privileges), and tours (a marching punishment). Otherwise, shooting was uneventful, which is surprising considering we were making a no-holds-barred subversive film in one of the most tightly controlled academic institutions in the country. Largely because of our right-under-your-nose assumption of permission and maintaining strict control over our script, we were never questioned. At no point did anyone try to shut us down. We hid our agenda in plain sight.

The 007-style cast included Cadet Bond; his beautiful associate, Domino; his high-tech outfitter, "Q;" General "M," and of course, an arch-nemesis, Alvin Blowfeldt. In our film, Blowfeldt enjoyed the double distinction of having been a member of the first USAFA class, class of 1959, and the first cadet ever to be kicked out for an honor code violation. Now, 25 years later, he had returned with a vengeance, killing cadets indiscriminately to the dismay of academy law enforcement. So Cadet Bond dutifully answers the call and saves the day – the simple plotline merely providing a framework for the placement of a series of inside jokes. The jokes had, in fact, been written first.

Any filmmaker will tell you that, in spite of or because of the labors and joys of the filmmaking process, the true reward of the experience comes with the screening of the finished product – there's nothing quite like observing the audience reaction. I had set the screening date for the evening before graduation, in part to celebrate graduation and in part to give the administration little opportunity to retaliate before I would be safely on my way to my first assignment, undergraduate navigator training.

We had posted fliers around campus and aired a short, radio-style advertisement over the public address system to promote the world premier. I had secured a large lecture hall that seated about a thousand, and set up my projector as the audience began to trickle in. Within minutes, every seat was taken and cadets began to sit in the aisles. When the aisles were full, they gathered in the open doorways to watch, some standing on overturned trash containers to see over the heads of those crowding the doorways.

As the film started, so did the laughter, and my spirits swelled with pride. The laughter continued through the film, right up to the end, after which everyone shuffled back into the real world.

And that's how, on one of the tightest budgets in history, at one of the most oppressively controlled institutions in the country, I made a satire of cadet life, got off scot-free, and had the time of my life doing it. The very next day, President Reagan shook my hand and gave me my diploma. I tossed my wheel-cap into the air and started my real life.

Through all the victories and defeats that make up a human life, this experience stands out as one of my finest moments. If you ask me who I *really* am, no matter how I respond, I'll likely be *thinking* about the cadet showing that movie to a packed house.

Part Two: Slowly I Wake

The months passed and I did not write. March turned to April. April gave way to May, then June and July... and still I did not write. I had nothing to say. Uninspired, in pain and convinced by several experiences that my mind had been permanently compromised, I languished in bed as the days spread into weeks and months. Then something amazing happened – I felt better. Gradually I realized that my inspiration to write had not left me, but rather changed into something different. Where I had been writing about death, I must now engage the topic of life. I was going to survive, and it might be good to explore "living."

Chapter 14: The Politics of Illness

As I write this it is August 5, 2006 – over seven months into my treatment for AIDS, and I feel better – "better" in this case being a measure of general well-being that includes my physical condition, an apparently unscathed intellectual capacity and a fairly healthy emotional outlook toward the immediate future. I'm prepared to start writing again, and that, for me, means everything.

The recovery process was so gradual that it's only now – months later – that I can look back and say with confidence, "I'm much better."

Until recently, I'd never taken an IQ test, mainly because I've never given these tests much credence. I therefore had some trepidation in July when I decided to try it. I was still afraid that my mental capacity had been compromised by AIDS and the various illnesses I had dealt with, but my curiosity overcame the fear that had stopped me from continuing to work on this book. I found a resource online and, after I took a short test, it returned a score of 140, which did wonders for my self-confidence. A few weeks later, I tried another test and scored 141. The confirmation felt even better.

As I once again begin working on the book, I realize a difference in myself that is striking. My new self is not only less feeble of body and mind, but perhaps less poetic ("poetic" here referring to my state of mind rather than writing style). With my demise on hold for the moment, and my existence less tenuous, I feel less urgent. I now have more time – more in the way of options. It is odd indeed to realize that I am at once grateful to be returned to myself and sorrowful at the absence of a connection to the hereafter I had felt I was approaching.

In July, I went to my regularly scheduled appointment at the University of Texas Health Center Pharmaceutical Research Department to participate in the AIDS study. About a week later, my nurse phoned.

"Have you been ill?," she asked.

"No, why?"

"We need you to come back and re-do your blood work. I'm afraid your kidneys might be failing."

A few days later, I was back in an exam room at the University Health Center. After several painful attempts, the nurse had finally given up on her attempts to insert a catheter. Dr. Borucki sat down with me to explain that I had a dangerously enlarged prostate – so enlarged as to make inserting a catheter impossible. Without the benefit of a specialist's input, his best prognosis was that my kidneys could still be saved, but only if I had a timely operation.

Up to now, all the opportunistic illnesses I had suffered had been common enough to be classified as typical HIV-related issues, and had therefore been covered under various forms of public assistance. Even my hospital stay had been covered under Medicaid, the protection of which I enjoyed up until the day my disability benefits had started in April. Those benefits ended, however, the moment the government considered me legally disabled – the assumption being that disabled persons are eligible for Medicare. These regulations seem to ignore the mandatory two-year waiting period before newly classified disabled persons can receive Medicare benefits.

Nor were there any exceptions to the Smith County Indigent Health Care program application process, which automatically disqualifies disabled persons from receiving care.

Program after program politely informed me that disabled persons receive their medical benefits through the Social Security Administration.

So I called Social Security and told them my situation. "Are there any exceptions?," I asked.

"Yes," the claims representative explained. "After you've received a kidney transplant and are actively on dialysis, you may reapply under the "total renal failure" category, and there is no waiting period for health care for that type of disability."

I couldn't believe my ears. "But my kidneys can still be saved."

"I'm sorry, sir, but we can't help you till after they've been replaced."

I was in shock. "Does what you just said make any sense to you."

"I don't make the laws, sir, but I'm required to enforce them."

And she was right, of course. It's a pointless waste of effort to get upset with administrators over issues out of their power to change. I politely ended the call and left a message on my nurse's voicemail regarding my abysmal progress.

The local newspaper had recently run an article about the imminent closing of Jamieson Clinic, the sole source of public assistance for much of the local HIV population. The federal government had cut HIV treatment funding nationwide in an effort to keep the national deficit from spiraling further out of control. Another recent article explained how a bill before Congress intended to raise the national minimum wage slightly included a rider that gave a tax break to a few thousand of the wealthiest people in the country. Yet another bill sought to increase the budget for our war in Iraq.

So I find myself in an odd position. I can't save my kidneys because I have no health care insurance. I can't get private insurance because HIV makes me uninsurable. I'm not eligible for veteran's benefits because I'm gay. I'm not eligible for Medicare because I'm still in my two-year forced waiting period. I'm not eligible for anything else because I'm disabled.

In Chapter 7, I wrote optimistically about the convoluted methods of applying for assistance in the United States, likening the myriad programs, many of which are locally or regionally based and funded, to a "safety net." For many of us, remaining connected to this safety net is itself a full-time job, and even then, there are huge gaps in protection that threaten to be fatal.

My brother heard about a local clinic that serves uninsured people -- people, like myself, who fall between the cracks of eligibility requirements for Medicare or Medicaid and who either can't afford private insurance or who are uninsurable. Two friends had recommended the clinic to him. The clinic had helped one of them get major back surgery; the other received a delicate carpal tunnel operation.

It's a prominent free clinic with a good address right downtown, just behind one of the largest churches in Tyler. Walking into the lobby, I was immediately impressed with the cleanliness, size, and professionally designed logo – all in sharp contrast to Jamieson Clinic. Glancing through the brochure, I was impressed that the doctors were volunteers. There was a nominal fee of $10 per visit. My guess was that the clinic was funded by a local church or churches, since there was a chapel right next to the reception desk and the application asked twice about which church I was now attending. The application also asked about my HIV status.

I handed the completed application to the receptionist, who said that a nurse would see me shortly.

I had only been waiting on the large, comfortable sofa a few minutes when a nurse angrily walked up to me and loudly announced, "We don't see you people. I suggest you try here." She handed me a piece of folded paper. Inside she had written, "Jamieson Clinic."

She was already walking away when I stood and called after her, "I know… I mean I'm already a patient at Jamieson, and they're great, but they can't help me with this problem."

She stopped and turned very slowly. She made no attempt to hide the fact that she was now quite perturbed. "If you're already a patient there, you know that's just not true," she admonished. "What exactly is your medical issue? Wait, let's go in here to talk."

Up to this point, our conversation had been shouted across the lobby. The nurse now bade me to follow her into an exam room to speak privately. "OK," she said, "tell me exactly what's going on."

"Jamieson is an STD clinic," I said, "They're set up to help people with HIV and certain opportunistic illnesses common among HIV patients, but my doctor, Dr. Borucki, tells me that if I don't get an operation soon, my kidneys may be permanently damaged. His fear is that, without any assistance, it may not be possible to get medical care for this issue until I'm in total renal failure, and then it will be too late to save my kidneys."

The nurse watched me speak, making no attempt to hide her expression of utter contempt, as if she had caught me red-handed

THE REMAINDER OF MY LIFE

trying to steal health care from people who deserved it. "Now that's just not true, is it?," she said condescendingly.

"Look," I answered, still not fully comprehending why she seemed so angry, "I don't know what you think I'm trying to pull off here, but I promise you I'm not."

Finally, she smiled smugly. "Well, we don't work with you people here – that's what they're for," gesturing toward the piece of paper I held in my hand. "We couldn't help you with an operation anyway. We don't do operations here."

"I understand," I said. "Thank you for your time."

And I did understand. The whole truth of the experience finally hit me with full force as I walked out of the beautiful, well-appointed clinic. The nurse had not been angry with me for "trying to pull one over" on her. She had been angry because I had defiled the sanctity of her clinic. Into her pristine work environment, I had brought a disease created by God to cleanse the earth of its most reviled sinners. Not only had she avoided the use of any AIDS or HIV terminology, referring to HIV patients as "you people," she couldn't even bring herself to say the word "Jamieson" out loud, preferring to scratch out the name on a bit of paper.

There's an interesting psychology associated with being the victim of prejudice. The typical initial response to such treatment is shame – a feeling of being unworthy. For me, shame turned into outrage when I considered the larger community – my gay and lesbian brothers and sisters who are subjected to similar treatment. If they can treat me this way, then they are likely treating others the same way, and that's simply not acceptable. Arthur Dong, author of the award-winning documentary series "Stories from the War on Homosexuality," was asked to compare, in his personal experience, racial prejudice to anti-gay prejudice. He responded by saying that they are very different in that, unlike racial prejudice, anti-gay prejudice is actively approved and condoned by our government and by religion.

In 1993, 23-year-old Nicholas Ray West of Tyler, Texas made international headlines when he was brutally beaten and shot to death by three local assailants. The murder seemed especially heinous because of the attitudes and nonchalant recounting of the execution by the three men, who were arrested shortly afterwards. One man described the event in such a way that it was apparent he fully expected to be released when the police found out the victim had been gay. Another showed no fear of long-term incarceration, largely because he had been released in a previous murder case. The judge had dismissed the charges, apparently because he considered the killing of a "faggot" a victimless crime.

The three assailants were united in the beliefs that gay people typically carry more cash than straight people; that gay people carry with them too much shame to report an assault to the police; and that the police in Tyler were less likely to make an arrest in a crime against a gay person.

This last assumption, fortunately, proved to be false. Two of the men have since been executed. The third is serving a long prison term.

At least two documentaries were made as a result. "Lone Star Hate," made for the BBC; and "Licensed to Kill," a film by Arthur Dong. "Lone Star Hate" includes scenes and interviews from local churches, where pastors and parishioners alike nonchalantly speak about the evils of homosexuality, claiming that it's an abomination against God and a blight on the community. The churches don't actively form anti-gay lynch mobs, they just create an atmosphere that makes such mobs more likely to develop.

Tyler, Texas is not, I'm sure the worst place in the country for gays to live, but it remains a crucible of bias in which are evident the dangers of tacit compliance with institutionalized prejudice. Even the counselor who runs a local HIV support group warned during a recent session, "People in Tyler don't make waves," meaning the gay community here tends to remain closeted and silent.

Unfortunately, this silence only contributes to an already fertile breeding ground for hatred, prejudice and violence against the gay community.

There are many ways to "kill a faggot." Aside from going out and shooting them (not very politically correct), you can simply deny them health care. Tacit support of anti-gay prejudice is clear in the federal government's funding of "abstinence only" HIV programs, for which most of the funding goes directly to religious organizations – the same churches preaching that homosexuality is an abomination to God.

Denial of medical care is not, of course, a uniquely gay issue. Not only is HIV no longer a uniquely gay disease, but there seems to be a growing number of Americans with other health care needs who fall between eligibility gaps. One can't help but wonder how many of us die annually because there were no available options – the only comfort on the otherwise bleak landscape being that, once your kidneys have failed… once you're actually dying… you can always get "emergency room medical insurance," which is cost-effective and about as useful as a freeway to the moon.

Chapter 15: Sometimes... You Get What You Need

"But if you try sometimes you might find
You get what you need"
You Can't Always Get What You Want, the Rolling Stones

TODAY IS AUGUST 14, 2006. There is a new show on the ABC Family channel called "Three Moons Over Millford" that I found intriguing. The premise is that an asteroid has broken the moon into three large satellites, all now in a decaying orbit – meaning the end to all life on earth is near. So far, so good... it sounds interesting, but not very different from many other apocalyptic visions, right? Wrong. The difference in "Millford" is the widely disparate predictions by scientists around the planet regarding the timeframe: some give the earth six months; others twenty years; and still others believe science will develop a way to prevent the catastrophe altogether, buying the earth another billion years or so in the process.

The show intrigued me, since (whether intentionally or not) it forces its audience to consider what it might be like to live with AIDS. I'm not sure at this point whether the show will be popular, but it occurs to me that it likely would not have been made at all in a pre-AIDS world – that the scenario presented in "Three Moons" had not entered our collective consciousness before the AIDS epidemic. In one way, the broad set of possible outcomes ranging from six months to 20 years to a life span unaltered is not much different from the current human experience – not knowing when we are going to die is part of the human condition and is not unique to those with terminal illnesses or living under a fragmented moon. The difference lies solely in the vastly increased likelihood that the timeline is leaning toward the six-month option, and this seemingly small difference has a profound effect, both in real life and in the lives of the characters in the fictional show.

According to one character in the show, there are three common reactions that people have when confronted with the news of their possibly imminent demise. There's the "chicken littler," who panics, running around screaming that the sky is falling, trying to drum up sympathy and basically being useless. There's the "follow your dream-er," who abandons worldly responsibilities in favor of fulfilling lifelong hopes and dreams, such as travel or spiritual journeys. And finally there's the "muddle through-er," whose life seems largely unchanged after hearing the bad news. In the show, as in reality, the characters tend to defy those categories by assuming the characteristics of more than one of them.

The noblest of these personality types is the muddle-through-er, the person who remains at work and whose life is largely unchanged. Civilization, after all, depends on the muddle-through-er to keep the power on and to keep goods in the stores. If we were all follow-your-dream-ers or chicken littlers, disaster and collapse would soon follow.

The show is also interesting to me as an AIDS patient because it forces me to ask myself which personality type am I – and I suppose I'm a bit of all three. Writing a book is a lifelong dream of mine, yet I must remain firmly planted in the day-to day realities of making my way – planning to return to a local university to gain a more marketable skill set and associated degree (a bachelor's degree in psychology and a dollar will buy you a cup of coffee). At times, however, I suppose I'm a bit of a "chicken littler." Disheartened by politics and prejudice, I sometimes see the future as grim.

I'm especially worried about two trends that have emerged in American life in recent years – nationalism and fundamentalism. It strikes me that these may be the two most dangerous mindsets in the world. They are equally treacherous because both remove one's responsibility to reason. Nationalism gives rise to such sentiments as "America: love it or leave it," and "America, right or wrong." Nationalism makes a crime out of questioning the president's decisions, requiring citizens to support the decisions made for them.

For these people, it becomes a crime to think independently. Those who accuse critics of the war in Iraq of being traitors are suffering from the mental disorder called "nationalism."

Similarly, fundamentalism says those who truly believe the bible was written by God aren't allowed to question it. Accordingly, when a verse in Leviticus instructs righteous believers to kill all homosexuals, it becomes immoral to ignore it. Such religious followers cannot be reached with reason when they believe that God has made so clear His will.

The moral of this story is, don't subscribe to any mindset that diminishes your human responsibility to think for yourself. There are plenty of historical reasons to refuse blindly following any doctrine, dogma or leader -- as any surviving followers of Hitler or the Reverend Jim Jones could attest.

In this age of enlightenment, it seems odd that we gay people find ourselves at a standoff, unable to engage in meaningful dialogue with a religious group that doesn't believe we have the right to exist. How can we discuss marriage issues, military service or health care when the pervasive, unalterable premise on which the counterargument is built says that we don't have a right to live?

If that makes me a "chicken littler," so be it – though my remarks are written in the spirit of hope for change rather than prophesying doom....

There is nothing in my makeup or lineage that makes me particularly worthy of special consideration. I don't walk into a store, expect the masses to part and place me at the front of the line. I don't apply for health care and expect administrators to make an exception for my exceptional case. I don't demand special rights or privileges or ask to be treated better than the common person. No one does – it would be laughable or even absurd to think otherwise. If I may presume for a moment to speak for all gay people, I would say that we do, however, hope and expect to be treated as human beings, with the same rights and privileges that are afforded to others.

I don't deserve special consideration or treatment, but I got it. When the "safety net" of health care failed me, my physician, Dr. Borucki, intervened. The social worker from the University of Texas Health Center (UTHC) called to let me know that, in spite of the University's moratorium on new indigent care intakes, he had arranged for me to see a specialist under that program. Before this intervention, I was headed toward renal failure, dramatically diminishing my odds for survival.

My immediate reaction was one of thanks, followed quickly by guilt – thinking of countless others nationwide whose doctors may not be willing or able to provide such lifesaving interventions. I am not worthy of special treatment, but I got it anyway. How am I supposed to feel about that? Happy *and* sad – I suppose that's a natural response. It also says volumes about my doctor, whose care and compassion continue to amaze and humble me.

Having sick kidneys feels like… well… like someone punched me in the kidneys. It feels sore but not particularly painful. This aching sensation soon extends to my joints, so that I feel as though I've come down with the flu. I tire easily, spending much time in bed. The night sweats have returned, though not as severely. And all this, I must say, is still a vast improvement over the "un-wellness" I felt after beginning the HIV regimen – so I'm not complaining.

When Dr. Borucki first discovered my kidneys weren't functioning properly, he immediately took me off many of my prescriptions, which simplified my daily pill-popping routine. At this point, I'm down to Kaletra, hydrocodone (body aches), famitodine (stomach cramps), fluconazole (anti-yeast/antifungal), promethazine (nausea), Avodart (prostate/kidneys), and the two mystery HIV drugs that are part of the double-blind study for GSK.

My CD-4 count fluctuates these days between 180 and 230, a vast improvement from a count of seven cells on the day I began treatment. At the same time, my viral load has decreased dramatically from over a million to "undetectable."

Special Health Resources of East Texas, affectionately referred to as "SHRET," is a privately held corporation contracted by the state of Texas to coordinate services specifically for HIV patients. For each patient, SHRET provides a case manager as a primary point of contact through which medical, housing, transportation and other services may be accessed. Over the past several months, the value of such an organization has become increasingly obvious to me. I'm both thankful for them and hopeful that other states provide similar services.

About two months ago, I began attending weekly group sessions there, not because I felt I needed therapy but for the purpose of meeting even the smallest sampling of Tyler's hidden gay population. Besides, the group sessions at the Wellness Center had been shut down due to budget cuts. In spite of myself, I quickly discovered the meetings were highly therapeutic. It gave me an outlet for venting my frustrations and allowed me the opportunity to comfort and relate to others, all of which was good for my mental health.

I discovered that I had been suffering from a strange kind of withdrawal – "people" withdrawal. From owning a blues bar in North Carolina a few months ago to being cloistered in my tiny bedroom had been quite a shock to my system, and the group sessions at SHRET were just the medicine I needed to keep hold of my sanity.

There are currently eight to ten of us in the group, though only three to six of us show up at any given session. These patients are from widely varying backgrounds and age groups, but one young man in particular whom we'll call "Mark" quickly captured my heart and my sympathy.

Mark is about 25 years old. When I met him at his first visit to group, he was intensely nervous. The simple act of speaking seemed to require of him enormous willpower. His voice cracking under the strain, he seemed perpetually on the verge of breaking into great, agonizing sobs. His face bore an expression of unbearable sorrow. But he did not cry. He spoke slowly, deliberately, about terrible things, without shedding a single tear, as he gradually revealed his story.

Originally from Tyler, he moved to Seattle several years ago, taking with him all the dreams and ambitions of youth. He fell in love, and he and his partner got an apartment together, enjoying the promise of the bright lights in the big city. His partner did not mention to Mark that he had AIDS, and never made any attempt to make their sexual contact safe. It was only after Mark became ill and tested positive that his partner told him the truth. As if the situation weren't tragic enough, this same murderous partner quickly tired of the HIV-positive version of the man he had infected – growing distant and uncaring. So Mark did the only thing left for him to do. He returned home, to Tyler, to his mother's home – a mother who had told him that his being gay was not her problem – that he should never mention it to her again.

When I met him, Mark had resolved not to tell his mother he was positive. If she didn't want to hear he was gay, he reasoned, she surely wouldn't want to hear about his HIV status.

He was utterly alone -- no family with whom to share his burden and not a single friend in what had become for him a city of strangers. Nor did he have a doctor. In his depression, the complex landscape of health care access formed an impenetrable wall. So, he remained untreated. It seemed to me that he had resigned himself to his own death. And yet, after all he had been through, the worst part of his current experience was that his ex in Seattle had stopped returning his phone calls. This of all things was the hardest for him to reconcile. His heart was breaking. He was in agony and it was tough to hear his story.

I tried to convince him to tell his mom about his HIV status, but deferred to our group's moderator, who felt it best not to pressure him. We did, however, tell him about Jamieson Clinic and made him promise to make an appointment to get medical help.

Since then, Mark has begun treatment, though he remains inscrutable in his despair – he doesn't talk much in group and always seems just out of reach of our attempts to provide him with comfort. He is still attending the sessions, however, which gives me hope that he still holds out some hope for himself. More than anything, I wish for him a sense of camaraderie, that he may learn to reconnect to people in spite of the cruel blows he has been dealt.

We must all find our own way, I suppose. Living with HIV is a uniquely personal experience that we have to figure out for ourselves. There is no right answer, no approved solution. The follow-your dream-ers will find healing in a new spiritual journey; the chicken-littlers may be debilitated for a time by their own fears; and the rest of us will just muddle through the experience, grateful for each new dawn – with a single question on our minds: "What further wonders will this new day bring?"

For "Lisa," there will be no new days. Lisa passed away in a local hospital two months ago. I can only tell her story from a distance and in general terms, because those involved are rightly fearful for their jobs, should enough detail escape to allow the pointing of fingers.

By the time she appears in our story, Lisa was already in mortal danger. She had obviously endured great hardship when a family member brought her to a local HIV/AIDS support center. She was emaciated beyond starvation. Carrying her remaining 58 pounds on her 5'1" frame, she could barely walk, and her illness had rendered her attempts at speech unintelligible. Her family had brought her to the office to apply for health services after trying to get help from two different hospitals. In each case, the hospitals had turned her away saying, "We aren't equipped to treat her."

I don't believe the hospitals were suggesting they weren't equipped to treat dehydration – it would be a sad hospital indeed that had no facilities to provide intravenous fluids. They were simply saying that they preferred not to treat patients with AIDS.

Which brings us back to the support center and a 27-year-old woman whom I never met, sitting with a family member who was asking for help. It had, in fact, required Herculean effort for her to walk into the office. Lisa was dying.

The compassionate office worker took Lisa's application for assistance, but urged above all else that she go to a hospital immediately. Lisa's need for medical care was obvious and urgent.

This all took place on Friday. On the way home after work, the office worker decided to swing by the hospital to check up on Lisa's progress. She found Lisa in a comfortable room, hooked up to an IV. She even managed to coax from her a feeble smile. At last, Lisa was receiving some care, though her recovery would be long. The office worker felt better, at least, about Lisa's odds for survival.

But on her way out, the office worker stopped by the nurse's station and was horrified to discover they were processing Lisa's discharge paperwork! "This is crazy," she thought, as she pleaded with the charge nurse to reconsider Lisa's discharge. Her pleading seemed to have some effect, because Lisa was not discharged. The new plan was to keep her in the hospital through the weekend.

On Monday, the office worker called the hospital and was told the tragic news. Lisa had passed away on Sunday.

Lisa's story requires no analysis or explanation – no political framework or agenda. I have "sanitized" details as much as possible to protect the family's privacy and to protect the "office worker" as well as her office from reprisal. The specifics I have presented are true, and I present them here as a simple, if less than adequate, way to honor the memory of a young woman who was a human being, who lived a human life and whose story deserves to be heard.

Chapter 16: My Court Martial

In 1994, I spoke at a Parents, Family and Friends of Lesbians and Gays (PFLAG) meeting of 150 or so in the sanctuary of a large Methodist church. I've included the verbatim transcript of my presentation so that readers of this book can understand more fully the story of my court-martial and the position in which I and other gay people find ourselves today.

In preparing for my court-martial, my attorney arranged a psychological evaluation that was supposed to prove beyond any doubt that I was a normal, healthy heterosexual male. After a short interview, I was asked to remove my clothing, at which time an electrical device resembling a tinfoil tube was placed around my penis. I was then shown a series of slides depicting attractive males and females. The device, I was told, would measure even the smallest excitability in my penis as the slides progressed. It required all my concerted effort to try to respond in a way counter to my nature, but I apparently succeeded. After the test, I was informed I had "passed." The good doctor determined that I was, in all scientific certainty, not homosexual.

In retrospect, it is easy to see that my conviction was a foregone conclusion. I had been found guilty of sodomy before the actual trial ever started (the court made no distinction between proving that I was gay and proving that I had committed sodomy. Any person proven to be gay was obviously guilty of sodomy). Why, then, did the prosecution feel it necessary to manufacture a confession? To my bewilderment, and quite late in the trial, the prosecution suddenly "discovered" notes taken during my initial interrogation that suggested I had confessed to all charges. Neither the judge nor the jury seemed to think it odd that such an important piece of evidence had been omitted from mention before the last few days of the trial.

Of course, some may ask why I would be so put off by a prosecutorial lie when my entire defense was based on the false proposition that I was not gay – but I was still naïve enough about the depths of prejudice to be surprised at such an obvious deception on the part of the US government.

While many of the references (Keith Meinhold, David Mixner, Bill Clinton, and others) are somewhat dated, a modern reading reveals the politics of my talk at the Methodist church is both intact and timely. As predicted, far from easing pressure on gays in the military, the "Don't ask, don't tell" policy has resulted in more dismissals than ever. To understand why, read on:

I AM AIR FORCE CAPTAIN TROY CARLYLE, and I was court-martialed in 1993 for being gay, based on the testimony of one person. In spite of the testimony of nearly

30 defense witnesses, I was convicted, and faced nine years in a military prison.

My career was obviously destroyed, though I was an AF Academy graduate with a spotless service record, had been awarded the Air Medal w/Oak Leaf Cluster (among other medals and honors), and served in a prestigious position with the highest possible security clearance at the time I was accused.

I was also a foster parent, a writer/filmmaker, and founder of an artist's support organization called Independent Filmmakers of Fayetteville.

There are many ironies in this story, but in order to relay more of the full impact, perhaps I should provide some groundwork:

The struggle of gays in the military may seem far removed from most of our relatively peaceable lives here in Houston, but it has wide-sweeping effects on all gays and lesbians throughout the country. I think Randy Shilts put it best in his book, *Conduct Unbecoming: Gays and Lesbians in the U.S. Military*. In this passage, Randy writes of the dangers inherent in excluding gays and lesbians from the armed services:

"Such policies make it known to everyone… that lesbians and gay men are dangerous to the well-being of other Americans; that they are undeserving of even the most basic civil rights. Such policies also create an ambivalence in which discrimination, harassment, and even violence against lesbians and gays is tolerated and to some degree encouraged."

This is a tale of witch-hunts -- about blind fear and the mindless damage it inflicts. It's a story about an inquisition-style military justice system firmly anchored in political agendas -- a lop-sided beacon aimed at proving accusations, instead of discovering truth. It's a story about a country and a people who went to a rally and then forgot why they were there. It's a story about people and families and lives irreparably damaged by a machine too big or too cold to notice or care. Finally, it's a story about loyalties and decisions, and realizing perhaps too late the value of a timely coming out party.

My story starts on the evening of June 2, 1992, I was 30 years old, but had only been "out" to myself, and selected friends and family members for about three years. Ironically, during that same three years, I had been serving in one of the most elite and secretive flying units in the Air Force, known cryptically as "Credible Cat," or simply "Special Activities." During this time I had "come out" to only one other military person -- a pilot in the same unit whom I called "Lex." Lex and I were comrades and best friends and eventually housemates, but never once had sexual relations. Though he had admitted to me an interest in "experimenting" with being gay, he claimed to be, at most, bi-sexual and was much less comfortable with people knowing his sexual orientation than I. But despite Lex's having only been even semi-out for about a year (two years less than me) and despite his self-admitted only "slight" attraction to men, it was Lex who had first found a lover and found himself in a relationship of sorts. I used to kid him that he was gayer than I was. He used to kid me that I was just playing the field.

Lex first met Richard at one of my film club meetings, and they became fast friends and lovers. But gradually Lex became uncomfortable with Richard's frequent unscheduled visits. Richard was spending too much time at the house, he feared, and someone just might figure out his emerging sexuality.

It might help to remember here the atmosphere in the country at the time. The elder Bush was President, candidate Bill Clinton had not yet announced his intention to lift the ban on gays in the military and the occasional article in the local North Carolina newspapers about gays in the military shed no real hope of imminent changes. The name "Keith Meinhold[4]" had only begun to appear in the press. In short, it paid to be discreet.

Lex tried to explain to Richard that he was in fear for his career as a pilot, and asked for some breathing space.

---

[4] Keith was a naval airborne sonar analyst and instructor who was discharged in 1992 after announcing on an ABC television news program that he was gay.

We even began joking about what the military might do if we were found out, but Richard didn't seem to catch on -- in fact, Lex's attempts to distance himself from Richard only seemed to serve to make Richard more desperate for his attention. I think eventually, Richard began to suspect Lex must have fallen for someone else. Richard became immediately very cold to me, and Lex caught him on occasions looking through his bedroom window. Mysteriously, broken planters, overturned garbage cans, and other incidents around our home occurred with increasing regularity.

June 2, 1992

Lex had gone out, and I had gone to bed early. I don't know if I can recall ever being awakened from a sleep as sound as the one I was enjoying the next morning. Lex was shaking me and was, as the fog cleared enough for me to make out his face, himself shaken. He told me someone had vandalized his restored TR-6 British racing car. The crime had been committed in the early hours of the day, and the perpetrator had long-since vanished. I asked him if he knew who had done it. "Who do you think," was all he said. By the time I arose that morning, Lex had already departed on a short overnight Air Force mission, and I went out to see the damage. Lex's prize-winning showpiece had been spray-painted inside and out.

Even the meticulously restored wooden dash had been painted. The seats had been slashed; the gas cap removed, and I saw several empty salt containers and a funnel on the ground. As I walked around the rear of the car, I saw the word "FAG" spray-painted over the license plate.

June 4, 1992

Upon arrival at the interrogation room, I was informed that I was not under arrest. I was read my rights, and was asked if I wanted to see a lawyer. I told the agents I had nothing to hide, and wanted to cooperate in any way I could. During the following interrogation, I was told that my housemate (Lex) and I had been accused of committing the crime of sodomy with Richard Bullock, and that we were facing up to ten years in prison. (Sodomy, under the Uniform Code of Military Justice, is also punishable as "conduct unbecoming of an officer.") Richard had apparently given the Office of Special Investigations (OSI) a nine-page report of alleged sexual contact between himself, and both Lex and me. It was obvious by the agent's tone and actions that this was a deadly serious matter, and I was apparently in a lot of trouble.

Toward the end of the three-hour ordeal, I was told I needed to sign a consent form for the agents to search my house. When I told the agents I wanted to see a lawyer, they became very angry, stating that asking for a lawyer constituted "uncooperative" behavior. They told me that, if I insisted on seeing an attorney, I would probably never fly again, I would lose my job as a navigator and that I would most likely be assigned to lawn-mowing or painting duty. One of the OSI agents stated further that if I wanted to be able to hold my head up, that I would admit to everything and allow them to search my house. I assured him that I had no trouble holding my head up.

The agents angrily returned me to my commanding officer's (Colonel Southerland's) office, where I was introduced to a male lieutenant who was to be my guard. Though no charges had been filed and I had not technically been placed under arrest, the lieutenant was ordered to drive me home in an Air Force vehicle (I was not allowed to take my car home); to keep constant watch over me, even when in the bathroom (this under the guise of a suicide watch); to make sure that I didn't remove anything from the house; to make sure I didn't try to operate my computer or VCR; and finally, to make sure that I didn't try to contact anyone, especially Lex, who was about to return from a cross-country mission.

Meanwhile, Lex was about to undergo similar treatment. He landed at about 11:00 p.m., and was met at the plane by Colonel Southerland, who claimed that, though it was late and raining, he felt that he needed to meet more aircrews at the time of landing in order to keep in touch with the workforce better. He then asked Lex to accompany him, ostensibly to discuss his refusal of the pilot retention bonus. (Lex had refused because he planned to separate from the military later that year.) Colonel Southerland immediately drove him to a parked car, from which the same two plainclothes OSI agents emerged. As the colonel turned Lex over to the agents, he offered, "I'm sorry to have to do this."

Lex was driven to the same cubicle and interrogated in similar fashion for about 45 minutes, the only difference being that he was informed that I had told them everything -- that I had sold him out -- and had authorized a search of my part of the house. "Troy has cleared his conscience," they claimed, "and is at home right now sleeping soundly. You can make things a lot easier for yourself by doing the same. If you refuse to cooperate, you're going to watch everything you've worked so hard for all these years go down the drain. I've got your future in my hands," the agent said, "I can make you or break you and I suggest you cooperate"

At about 12:30 am (Friday, 5 June), the agents entered our house. One of the agents asked the lieutenant if I had tried anything, or had acted strangely in any way, and the lieutenant answered "No." The agents then relieved the lieutenant of his guard duties, and the three left my house.

A few seconds later, Lex entered and told me of his (similar) ordeal.

June 5, 1992

After a long, sleepless night, we found a lawyer (Mark Waple) and heard the first words of encouragement since our ordeal had begun. Mark felt we had a strong case with a good chance of winning. "Note very carefully the way I phrase my questions to you," the lawyer said. "At no time will you hear me ask whether or not you actually committed sodomy or any other crime. Before I take your case, however, and to make sure we don't run into any conflict of interest issues, I want to make sure you both intend to fight this in the same way."

I asked Mr. Waple what he meant, and he said, "Quite simply, that you're both fighting this as straight men, unjustly accused."

I asked, "What if a client was to fight charges like this as a gay man, unjustly accused." Lex immediately grabbed my arm and began leading me out of the room. "Well," Mark said, I don't think such a client would stand nearly as good a chance. A military jury would see an admission of being gay as being equivalent to an admission of committing sodomy."

Lex had had enough. In an adjoining office he admonished, "What are you trying to do? Troy, I can't do this. You don't know my family. I couldn't live with this. Its one thing if you decide to come out, but if you do this, you'll be dragging me down with you."

So, this was our division, and during the course of the following year and a half, while the government was preparing their case against us, it was the thing that would gradually tear our friendship apart. I never stopped wrestling with this issue, but in the end always found myself bound to the loyalty of my one-time best friend.

In other words, I would lie. I would lie throughout the course of the upcoming months as we worked together to reinvent our history and throughout my trial. I would come to justify these lies in my mind by imagining myself a Jew in Hitler's Germany being interrogated by Nazis. I rationalized that I wouldn't condemn a Jew for denying his religion to avoid prison, or worse... but there were other forces at work in my heart that told me I was about to betray countless others....

As we left our lawyer's office that afternoon, our work was laid out for us. In addition to calling various friends and family for the purpose of reconstructing a "heterosexual" past, we spent the next day trying to figure out how to raise the roughly $30,000 apiece in estimated attorney's fees. As for my part, I left both my mother and 90-year-old grandmother in tears after explaining over the phone why I needed (for the first time since leaving home 13 years prior) to borrow money.

By the time we went to bed Friday night, neither of us had been able to eat any solid food in 36 hours. I felt nauseated and disoriented. Our lawyer had advised us that, given our security level, we should proceed as though our house, cars and phones had been wiretapped. Two days prior, I had had a great job, established a separation date from the military, an attractive monetary bonus, and a job lined up. Suddenly, everything had been turned upside down, my security was gone and the organization I had served and grown to love had seemingly and without justification closed itself completely to me.

There are many reasons my court martial was "unjust" -- but the real tragedy here is one that even the national media has been reluctant to address; that these acts are not crimes. The whole premise of this type of "crime" is wrong. Two consenting adults sleeping together have not committed a crime in doing so. Let me say that again: Two consenting adults sleeping together have not committed a crime in doing so.

The only "crime" that occurs in cases like this is the institutionalized injustice embodied by the continued persecution of innocent people. As human beings, we should all be ashamed that we have allowed it.

THE REMAINDER OF MY LIFE

At the Air Force Academy, I learned that there exists a higher calling than the law -- that there have been times in history when we have learned that it's not always good enough to simply follow orders. I was taught to make my conscience my guide, and to beware of orders and rules that are themselves immoral or wrong.

During the last few weeks and months of my Air Force career, I saw many of the officers I once respected most, whether out of prejudice or fear of reprisal, sanction the purposeful and biased destruction of careers and futures of innocent people without any regard to dignity or basic human rights -- and we all know that Lex and I aren't the only ones. Let's start counting the innocent victims of laws against sodomy (laws against being gay) who are currently serving time in this nation's civilian and military prisons. According to C. Dixon Osburn, the co-director of the Servicemembers Legal Defense Network, the current "don't ask - don't tell" policy on gays in the military is only making matters worse:

"People will receive harsher penalties. More people are going to go through the criminal justice system than the administrative system and end up in jail. Given that they are not asking if you are gay but if you are involved in gay behavior, they are eliciting information punishable under the code of military justice."

In doing so, we use the same language that has always been used to justify the unjustifiable and inhumane crimes committed by society. Was it so long ago that we convicted women for trying to vote, and blacks for trying to sit at the front of the bus, or using the wrong fountain? Was it so long ago (try 1972), when the federal government finally ceased a 50-year-old policy of sterilizing young men and women for being stupid or "socially unfit?" Is it, then, really so hard to believe we are still persecuting gays and may continue to persecute gays?

At the Air Force Academy, I was taught that the difference between the Americans and the Germans during WWII is that we have an underlying morality to which we are held more responsible than to the law. This explains the Nazi war-crime trials, and why we tried our own Vietnam veterans for atrocities committed against civilian women and children, even though these officers were following orders.

In the same way, men and women in this nation's military are now following orders, and I'm here to tell you the military has committed hundreds of atrocities, very literally destroying the lives of innocent people in all branches. One of the smaller ironies in my case is that the assistant prosecutor against me was 1Lt Lorraine Bray. Lorraine argued for me to be imprisoned for being gay,

THE REMAINDER OF MY LIFE

saying "He walked [into that gay bar] and he left everything else outside. He abandoned those things he was taught to treasure at the Air Force Academy; his beliefs in duty, and honor, and country, the idea that we uphold and live to a standard of conduct that we're all supposed to conform to - - are out there on the steps when he walked into [that gay bar]." But the irony is that Lorraine was merely performing her duty as my prosecutor. She didn't want to be there. She confided later that her own sister is gay. And as my mother pleaded to the jury not to send me to prison, Lorraine wept. It is my great hope and pride that our nation is currently undergoing changes that will correctly label the actions of this type of investigation and punishment as unjust and inhumane.

I predict a time in the future when the rights of homosexuals will be protected, and a time in the more distant future when our constitution will be correctly interpreted to apply to all people, not just the particular groups, such as blacks and women, who have so valiantly fought and paid so dearly to achieve legal recognition as human beings with human rights.

I would now like to briefly address the topic of guilt by association. The presumption made by my prosecution that underlined their philosophy in proving my guilt was that I must be a homosexual because some of my friends were homosexuals. Well, I've got news for them. To paraphrase David Mixner[5] in an introduction of Bill Clinton to a group of gay supporters prior to his election, "Homosexuals are our acquaintances, our neighbors, our comrades in arms, and they are our sons, our daughters, our mothers, our fathers, our brothers and our sisters." If association makes anyone guilty of this horrible crime, then my friends, we would all be guilty.

After I was convicted, I received my copy of the government's response to my appeal. The government's position in defending their conviction of me based on my association with gays was to say it's perfectly legal for the government to pass laws against association by military members with certain groups of people. As an example, they cited the 1980 case of Blameuser v. Andrews, which upheld an order placing white supremacist groups off-limits to military members.

Now, maybe I'm crazy, but there seems to be a bit of circular logic going on here. It's OK to make association with gays illegal since its OK to make association with white supremacists illegal. In other words, it's OK to exclude people who practice hate, so therefore it's OK to

[5] David Mixner was and remains a rock in the American Civil Liberties movement. Beginning with volunteer work for John F. Kennedy in 1960, he "came out" as part of his fight against Anita Bryant's attack on gay rights in the 1970s. His new book "On the Edge" will soon offer his take on the current state of freedom in America.

exclude people who practice love? And how many years do we have to go back when the military *was* a white supremacist group; and didn't their arguments against blacks in the military sound a lot like their argument against gays: "What about morale, what about the showers?"

But there is another insidious and dangerous thing that happens when we choose to determine guilt by association, as it becomes important to consider that, historically, guilt by association has been the primary criterion used to convict innocent people of acts that are not crimes. What easier way to convict a heretic during the Spanish Inquisition, a witch in old Salem or a communist under McCarthy's watchful eye than by pointing to condemned family members and friends?

And it never seems to occur to us that the reason we must rely on the technique of guilt by association -- the reason it is so hard to prove guilt otherwise -- is that we're not actually trying a person's deeds, but rather his or her thoughts, beliefs, or feelings.

In case you still find this hard to believe, my former commander at Credible Cat, Col Victor Powers, sat on the witness stand during my trial and told the judge he knew I was guilty because I had let him borrow "On The Road," by Jack Kerouac, and that he had warned me that this wasn't the kind of book a professional military officer should be reading. It saddens and frightens me to realize that

McCarthyism and witch-hunting are still alive and well and that thoughts and feelings can still be illegal in our nation and in our military.

Just as we saw McCarthyism destroy so many lives, friends are still coerced to testify against each other, and the pressure exerted is sometimes so great that names of entirely innocent people are given in a desperate attempt to escape punishment, or embarrassment, or degradation.

I have faced nine years in prison, the future of my best friend hanging in the balance, and my own case is still in appeal. I speak to you today against the advice of counsel, my friends, and the military establishment as one of the people in this country who perhaps can least afford to speak on behalf of the gay and lesbian community.

My challenge, then, to every American who values freedom and justice is that if I'm willing to speak my mind, then perhaps you can too.

I would like to read to you an excerpt from the closing arguments made by the prosecutor in my trial. The language is graphic, but I think it's helpful for us all to understand what we're up against, especially since this is a direct quotation from a very recent government proceeding against a member of the gay community. The following remarks concluded the prosecutor's closing statements at the end of my two-week trial:

"And why [were Captain Carlyle's lies perpetuated through this trial]? It was... because [they were] consistent with the character you've heard him to be from Lt Col Powers; a man of situational ethics, following Jack Kerouac in doing what he wants to do for himself."

"What would drive this man to go to this length to cover up his crime? ... Maybe it's the memory of Richard Bullock's penis going in and out of his mouth as he applied deep suction.... Maybe it's that notion which could drive the defense -- a calculated defense of this magnitude."

I have learned that you don't have to be gay to recognize that society's treatment and intolerant attitude toward gays and lesbians is itself intolerable, and I have come to believe through the course of my own court-martial that you don't have to be guilty to be convicted. It could happen to anyone. The Air Force has taught me that.

I am here to implore our nation and you present today to stop reassuring ourselves that the continued persecution of any person or group of people is morally justified, because it is not.

Even within our own gay and lesbian culture, we frequently don't hesitate to condemn our brothers and sisters. One of the most common arguments I hear against gay activism by both gays and straights is "I don't care what you are; do you have do go on parades and on TV and tell the world you're gay? I don't want to see that stuff, why force me to look at it? I don't go around telling the world I'm straight!" Well, I didn't tell the world I was gay. I had in fact only just discovered that fact for myself. I was hunted down and dragged out of the closet in the *New York Times* and on national television and in a tragic courtroom where my life was forever changed.

Maybe it's time this country takes a good hard look at itself and realizes we are not a country of straight white males but a country of people of all kinds. Until we can see the diversity, we can't learn to appreciate what we have. So maybe until things change, parades and TV and bumper stickers and "National Coming Out Day" and friends and family and people like those in this room are all we have.

After a long series of lies that have created in me a wound as deep as my soul, I can tell you my spiritual lesson from all this: When we were children, our parents taught us that we should speak the truth even when it hurts. My lesson is simply this: We must speak the truth... *especially* when it hurts. Therein, and only therein, lies our path to freedom. Believe me, I know. In protecting my friend, I betrayed countless others. This is a heavy weight I will forever have to bear.

What can we do? I've got a good start for you... The next time you see injustice, stop being a silent witness.

Stand up for yourself and for our brothers and sisters and speak the truth - the truth that says our freedom is not sacred in spite of our diversity, but *because of it.*

This country was founded on the concepts of freedom and religious rights. I think it's time we remind the Religious Right that it was tolerance they sought when they came to America. But we also must remind ourselves that it's tolerance the splintered and fractured gay, lesbian and transgender communities seek here and now. What do you say we all practice what we preach?

Chapter 17: Backlash

I WAS NERVOUS about seeing the urologist. Dr. Borucki felt my need was urgent – that without a timely operation, my kidneys might lose their ability to repair themselves. In addition, the financial "arrangements" that had been made were somewhat suspect. Since I had no medical insurance, Dr. Borucki somehow slid my appointment under the radar of hospital administrators. If for any reason I was to miss my appointment with the specialist, there could be no guarantee that I would be rescheduled.

I rolled over and through sleepy eyes noted the time on my bedside clock, 6:45 – and sheer panic ensued. My appointment was at 7:30, and I had a forty-minute drive ahead of me. I threw on my clothes and ran to my step-dad's room to borrow the car keys.

"It's Sunday," he said, barely awake. "Your appointment is tomorrow."

On Monday, August 21, I signed in at the hospital at 7:15. "Is there anything I need to fill out?" I asked.

"Let me see," the receptionist replied, "Who is your insurance carrier?"

It's an odd feeling, being at the mercy of the kindness of strangers. For one thing, it makes one extremely grateful for assistance. But it also creates a strange kind of nervous fear – the realization that care may be withdrawn at any time and with no rationale necessary. This distinct form of existence as a kind of invisible patient rose to the surface during the first few moments of my interview with the urologist.

A very young-looking doctor hurriedly entered the exam room and flipped through my records. He seemed puzzled.

"Why, exactly, are you here," he asked at length.

"Doctor Borucki felt it was an emergency," I answered, as I spilled coffee all over myself and the floor.

"Well, I certainly don't see anything in your records to indicate you've got any kidney problems."

"But Doctor Borucki felt I might even lose my kidneys if I don't get an operation soon," I pleaded, as I gathered paper towels to clean up the mess.

Finally, the urologist agreed to schedule me to come back in two weeks for a battery of tests to determine what, if any, problems I might have.

I breathed a sigh of relief -- I was still in the system.

I stopped by the out-processing table on my way out. "Is there anything you need from me?" I asked.

The young representative responded, "We just need your insurance information."

Now it's Wednesday, August 23, 2006. The hospital never called back to set my appointment for the tests the urologist had ordered two days ago, so I called to check in. Sandra tells me that she's not authorized to set an appointment until I can guarantee payment. As I had feared, my tenuous relationship with the urologist has slipped through the cracks.

I ask Sandra to talk with the hospital's social worker, which she agrees to do. She promises to do all she can to help and hopes to know more by the end of the week.

I can't help but wonder how my book will end – as a brush with disaster with hopeful promise; or perhaps finished by another author who describes my untimely demise as the byproduct of circumstances that left the health care system few choices but to deny services to one without sufficient insurance. Having expressed the question, I should assure the concerned reader that, at this point in time, I fully intend to write my own epilogue.

In 1992, just after my court martial, I moved from Fayetteville, North Carolina to Wilmington, a beautiful town on the Atlantic coast, to open a restaurant with Daniel, my partner in life and business. There I met a man by the name of Jim Bath. Jim, a septuagenarian, was (and remains) somewhat of a local legend. Jim is a wispy, bearded man whose long, stringy grey and unkempt hair floats down between his bony shoulder blades. Smoking a pipe, he looks like a character out of *Treasure Island*, and he eschews air conditioning and running water to live in various sheds and trailers provided by benefactors. Jim is a sailor, a pilot, an adventurer, a consumer of life. He has traveled the world and has frequently found himself at the center of grand movements. He is known by many celebrities and common folk and he is adored by all who know him. I was fascinated with his stories of 1950s San Francisco and his recollection of running into a fledgling beat generation – Jack Kerouac, William Burroughs, Allan Ginsberg, et al.

In 1992, however, Jim was the talk of the town for a different reason. His new riverside open-air bar, the Icehouse, was ground zero for a musical renaissance in Wilmington. In its short history, it had become nationally famous, garnering a segment on CNN and drawing major blues and rock talent (along with huge audiences) and igniting in downtown Wilmington a grand revitalization of food and culture. What had previously been a seedy ghost town began to vibrate with energy as an eclectic combination of restaurants, nightclubs, shops, and condominiums began to proliferate. (Years later, Jim would be instrumental in forming the design and charter for my own bar, The Rusty Nail, which I created following the Icehouse model. Jim introduced me to the Cape Fear Blues Society and even helped decorate the interior.)

Ironically, as the word spread and as an increasing number of people began to call the downtown area home, so did an increasing number of them begin to complain about the "noise" coming from Jim Bath's famous Icehouse.

Many airports have experienced the same phenomenon, which is called "encroachment." Many people want to live near airports for ease of transportation – that is, until they get there. Once planted near the object of desire, they petition to have it shut down. Historically, these bizarre power plays have been successful, as many shut down and relocated airports indicate.

Such was the case with the Icehouse. Within a few years of its opening, new condominium owners petitioned to shut down the very phenomenon that attracted them to Wilmington in the first place. Some of us tried to save the Icehouse from this fate. I helped form the Cape Fear Hospitality Association and served as vice president, but quickly discovered that other business owners, perhaps jealous of the Icehouse's patronage, weren't very motivated to help.

These days, the Icehouse is just a fond memory. Even the historic building that housed it (an authentic icehouse) has been demolished to make room for more condominiums.

I share this story for the purpose of exploring an odd, yet almost universal phenomenon: Too much success breeds failure. This is the theory of "backlash."

I had long known about backlash in the business world, but I didn't realize how it worked with gay rights until I got into gay history. I have been reading prolifically – a practice I took up about a month ago in clinic waiting rooms. The books are remarkable and are worth mentioning here as they all touch to some degree on the subject of this book. Interestingly, they have also raised in my consciousness the awareness of certain cycles in gay history, allowing me to place my personal experiences within a larger context.

Rescuing the Bible from Fundamentalism and *Living in Sin?* are two books by Episcopalian Bishop John Shelby Spong. The books propose a compelling argument in favor of a modern, thinking person's understanding of biblical texts. He points out many biblical standards we no longer consider relevant, such as dietary restrictions, polygamy and other bizarre familial sexual mores, such as the apparently sacramental union between Lot and his daughters. Biblical "literalists," he argues, are therefore actually forced to be "selective biblical literalists," picking and choosing which passages to take literally. These books were a revelation to me and helped me to view the bible once again as a viable (albeit non-literal) part of my life.

Jesus and the Shamanic Tradition of Same Sex Love, by Will Roscoe, is a well-researched survey of early religious practices throughout Europe and Eurasia. It was remarkable to discover an almost universal pre-Grecian tribal practice of tolerating and even holding in great respect certain same-sex unions. This custom was so pervasive that it remained a near-universal trait among American and South American tribes even as the first European explorers arrived. The many profound effects of Greek mythology on early Christianity are also explored in this groundbreaking book. It becomes impossible to digest this book without realizing its primary purpose – to make the reader aware that the time when Christ lived was a homophilic, not homophobic, era and raises the question, "What happened?"

Covering, the Hidden Assault on Our Civil Rights, by Kenji Yoshino is a powerful manifesto toward a better understanding of what it means to be gay or lesbian in the 21st century. Adroitly constructed, brilliantly conceived, it is a truly poetic vision that explains, at last, what's wrong with the gay rights movement, and how to fix it.

Out of the Past: Gay and Lesbian History from 1869 to the Present, by Neil Miller, is a carefully researched survey that actually takes enough time with each era to give the reader an authentic feel for the heroes and villains from our past. Most surprising was the realization of the cyclical nature of gay and lesbian freedoms during this period – we were more free to express same-sex love in the 1880s than we were at the turn of the century, more free in the 1920s and 1930s than in the 1940s. From the 1950s on, the wavering nature of sexual freedom seemed more pronounced. Alternately increasing and decreasing within a few years, the cycles came shorter and shorter. Frequently, our history is one of "two steps forward, one step back." Illustrated copiously, but with quotations and excerpts, rather than pictures – Miller's book should be mandatory reading for any student of civil rights.

The purpose of these book reviews is to provide a backdrop for my current insight. Since I first sensed that I might be gay, I have presumed that the history of gays progresses in much the same way as society at large. We can see a gradual improvement in living standards from cave dwellers to modern man. Similarly, on a scale of decades, we can see that standards are better today than they were 40 or 50 years ago.

Into this model I neatly placed the struggle for gay and lesbian equality, presuming we were far better off than we were two millennia ago, and somewhat better off than we were two decades ago. But alas, the model does not fit. Rather than the linear progression enjoyed by society at large, acceptance of gays by society at large looks more like a sine wave, curving upwards toward relative freedom only to turn downward once again toward further repression.

This brings us back to backlash – usually explained as a result of too much success at too rapid a pace. Even modest human-rights victories can bring about a mobilization of forces to nullify those victories, as was the case when several states actually passed laws forbidding same-sex unions after a few jurisdictions performed them for the first time. Every time we make significant progress, a puritanical interest seems poised to put it back in its place.

The model so eloquently proposed by Kenji Yoshino may be useful here in achieving for gay and lesbian culture a less fitful result -- suggesting we have perhaps been asking the wrong questions. Rather than being forced to justify our need for equal treatment, Yoshino says, perhaps we should demand that the other side explain in rational terms why gay rights need to be repressed. In other words, ask, "In what way will you be damaged by allowing me to live as a gay person?"

The solution will remain problematic. Fundamentalists have been socialized not to allow reason to cloud their thinking. Their selective literalism clutches the bible as if it were a life preserver, permeates the highest offices of our government with profound and often disastrous effects on our civil liberties. Nor is the problem unique to gays and lesbians. Any minority's successes may be significant enough to place them in the crosshairs. Jerry Falwell and many others used biblical literalism to preach in favor of continued segregation in the 1960s at a time when politics was moving to abolish that practice.

I was myself a religious fundamentalist for a short time as an Air Force Academy cadet, and remember being warned of anti-Christ types who might try to use clever rationality as a means to dissuade me from the one true path to righteousness. It became a simple task to tune out any conversation that smacked of challenge to my belief system. Ultimately, my attempt to ignore the contradictions between reality and my beliefs became too great a burden to bear. I could not turn off the world – so I chose instead to turn off my fundamentalism. In my defense, at no point during my fundamentalist period did I tell anyone they were a sinner, that God hated them or that they were going to Hell. Fundamentalism for me was an introspective exercise that I ultimately found to be incompatible with reality. But "fundamentalism" remains a hateful word, denoting beliefs that are responsible for much of the violence in the world. Islamic fundamentalists were responsible for the attacks on the World Trade Center on 9/11. Some Christian fundamentalists claimed this attack was God's punishment of a gay-tolerant America, then many of these same people cheered the unprovoked attack on Iraq. Another way to define fundamentalism is the irrational and anti-intellectual use of literal readings of selected ancient scriptures to justify the practices of discrimination and hate-mongering.

I have spent my life in thoughtful reflection… quietly contemplating the world around me, carefully considering people's motivations. I am an armchair mediator – a calm intermediary between rival parties… analyzing repercussions, avoiding conflict and loathe to hurt anyone's feelings. I am always first to turn the other cheek and last to lose his temper.

But I am angry.

I'm angry at America for reelecting Bush. I'm angry that I have been marginalized. I'm angry at the fundamentalist rantings that insist I remain marginalized. I'm tired of the people who shout from the treetops "God hates fags." I'm angry that the religious right acknowledges no responsibility for the crucifixion of Matthew Sheppard. I'm angry at the prevailing attitude that the only way to preserve family values is to destroy "undesirable" families. I'm angry at the homogenized and sanitized picture of the white picket fence and 2.5 kids as the only path to righteousness. I'm angry at the notion that my life is anybody else's business – that my very existence somehow threatens someone else's existence. I'm angry at our collective history. I'm angry at the hate-mongers on pulpits and soapboxes, shaking their fists defiantly against reason. I'm angry with people who think their humanity is more valuable than mine is. I'm angry that my order to appear at my court martial was stamped, "By order of the President of the United States," at a time when President Clinton had already announced he was going to sign an executive order that allowed gays in the military. Persecute me if you must, but don't do it in Clinton's name. I'm tired of lies and misquotes. My God never said that homosexuality was a sin – and neither did yours.

I'm tired of the age of ignorance – an age where it is moralistically pure to be stupid, and quite suspect of satanic influence to be smart. "Let's all hearken back to a simpler age when blacks were slaves and queers kept quiet. Those were the days." I'm angry at being vilified and blamed for the corruption of youth and the destruction of morality. What if all the gays moved out and you discovered that your children were even more corrupted and family values even more eroded? What if you discovered that the real evil influence has always been the very hate you preach? You have ironically caused the thing you ostensibly railed against: the decline of civility. Would you then invite us back? Would you then seek our guidance, our counsel? Or would you cry that we were still the root of your evil. Would you then, rather than turn to introspective reevaluation, call for our summary execution?

I'm angry for those who have gone before me – for the police raids and the public humiliations, of the lives ruined. I'm angry for the war heroes who were denied benefits because of who they loved.

I'm angry for those who are yet to come – yet to be murdered, and the purges yet to come. I'm angry that I will not in my lifetime see the end of oppression at the hands of zealots. I'm angry at the never-ending circular and contradictory "logic" used to justify hate and violence. Stop it, stop it, stop it, STOP IT!

While the religious right demands that I conform, my request for them is relatively simple. I don't expect to live forever. I am not afraid of dying. I do not feel all alone in the world. I do not regret my life. I do not demand to be cured, nor do I respectfully request that my country do everything in its power to extend my life as long as possible. Special treatment and medical care are not my birthrights, though if medical care is made available, I will certainly be grateful. I do not begrudge or covet the successes of others and I ask that the same consideration be made for me. I do not demand conformity from others, and I expect the same.

But I do want something, and it is more than tolerance. I wish for *acceptance*. "Tolerance" is an interesting word. It suggests we should not take action against others while implying we would like to. "Tolerance" presumes violent intent and that it is only by exerting extreme self-control that we inhibit violent actions. "Tolerance" is a state of self-coercion that always struggles toward intolerance. Accept me as I am – as God made me. Accept that all would be right in the world if only there were more acceptance. The line between tolerance and intolerance is too thin -- there is no liberty without acceptance.

Just because I don't understand how anyone could eat, let alone enjoy shrimp doesn't mean I have a moral imperative to stop others from eating shrimp. The fact that some people don't like shrimp does not give them the right to be angry with people who like shrimp; even if the bible says that eating shrimp is wrong, which it does, in Leviticus 11:12. On the other hand, the guy who loves shrimp DOES have a right to be angry if someone tries to stop him. And if we find ourselves tired and weary of talking about shrimp… always shrimp, enough shrimp, then WHY DON'T WE JUST LET THE POOR GUY ENJOY HIS SHRIMP! Otherwise, all of us are doomed to an endless debate over whether we should or shouldn't allow it.

I'm angry with "gay Republicans." How can anyone support a party that resists our most fundamental civil liberties? I am angry with all the closeted political spectators and participants who promote "change from within" while taking part in their own suppression. Change will come about only when we take ownership of who we are and demand angrily and with great passion to be treated as full citizens – as parents and as wives and as husbands – as children and teachers and doctors and politicians – as people who contribute and who need and feel and love… and love. We have an enormous capacity to love, and I am angry that the religious right insists on denigrating this profound and sacred state of being with their eternal fixation on sex – always sex. How small a part of who we are, how tedious and inane to make it always the central issue – how mindless and perverse.

I have a right – we collectively have a right – to be angry, and to use that anger to cry out against those who would diminish or extinguish us. We can make our anger a force to repel ignorance and the hatred it nurtures.

Chapter 18: The Small, Still Voice

I CLOSE MY EYES and try to think of nothing, listening for the music within the white noise. But today, I hear only noise. The faint rhythms elude me, the notes are indistinct. I listen intently for the small still voice that will tell me all is well. After all, if I were supposed to be somewhere else, I wouldn't be here. I believe in living under the presumption that my life represents the fulfillment of some purpose, and that it becomes my duty to ascertain exactly what that might be, so that I may proceed accordingly. There's no hoodoo-voodoo to it – it's a simple matter of faith that helps me stay focused on the important stuff. Today, that small voice is telling me to chill – to take a deep breath and return to my writing.

You may recall Shirley Cheisa, the lady from Tyler AIDS Services. I promised some months ago to do some volunteer work for her. I'll have my chance in late September – to sit at a table at the fair, answer questions and hand out literature. It will do me some good -- I'm looking forward to talking with people, and I'm looking forward to feeling useful.

Martin, a new friend I met in group, called to tell me about their need for people to staff the booth. Martin has been admirable in his efforts to reach out in friendship, and I am grateful – I have few acquaintances and fewer friends in Tyler. My libido, however, is nonexistent these days, due in part to my current medical condition, which includes dramatically reduced testosterone production. As I try to make new friends, I find myself being careful not to give the impression of romantic interest – trying not to hurt anyone's feelings.

I feel good. The miraculous effects of the protease inhibitors are evident when I look in the mirror. The gaunt face is gone, the pallor has been replaced by a healthy blush, I actually look a little younger than my years and people have begun to comment that I'm (gasp) attractive. The hand of death has been lifted from my shoulder, even if I'm not altogether well.

My parents live in a new, gated development of modest condominiums, strung neatly together in groups of four or five, with strict rules that prevent almost any type of landscaping or exterior personalization. The miniature community looks a little like a military base and seems to attract retirees primarily – in particular, people who lack the energy or interest required to maintain a lawn – people concerned about security – people who value conformity – older people.

They are a friendly bunch, however – neighbors are always greeted with a smile and a wave and no one is ever in too much a hurry to stop and chat.

I fit neatly into this group. Walking my dog at a pace slowed by stiff joints, I'm frequently overtaken by faster-moving senior citizens. My failing kidneys, while relatively painless, have transformed me into an older version of myself. I tire easily, so I take the opportunity to pause during my walk and chat with a neighbor. My next-door neighbor, Jack, has become my best friend. He's a diabetic Air Force retiree. We sit on his back porch and share military stories, or hospital stories, or talk about our dogs. Our best years behind us, we talk about our lives. It's an odd feeling... to just be one of the retirees. Thinking about it, I chuckle to myself that most people have to wait until they're sixty to be an "old fart." I'm well ahead of that schedule. I have fit much into this short life.

In 1895, Oscar Wilde was tried and convicted in England under the terms of the Labouchere Amendment, a law that prohibited male homosexual acts. He spent two years in prison, and died in France in 1900, a defeated, lonely and miserable man. His creative spirit, that flamboyant brilliance that marked him as one of the great writers, had been crushed. He never recovered. Many times in my life, I have wondered what great creative works the world has been denied because a few small-minded people felt the need to put Wilde in his place.

Oscar Wilde became a martyr of sorts. Within a few years of his death, his name invoked more than sympathy for the cause of decriminalizing consensual acts between adults of the same sex – it became a rallying cry for the birth of a movement toward equality.

In 1998, Houston police entered a private residence on a "false emergency call." Once inside, they arrested two consenting male adults in the act of having sex. The case went all the way to the Supreme Court, resulting in a landmark decision in 2003. "Lawrence v. Texas" is considered by many to be the most powerful gay rights decision in history. Overruling the 1986 opinion in Bowers v. Hardwick, the decision makes clear that privacy rights guaranteed by the Fourteenth Amendment apply to everyone. Justice Anthony Kennedy wrote the majority opinion in no uncertain terms: "The petitioners are entitled to respect for their private lives. The state cannot demean their existence or control their destiny by making their private sexual conduct a crime." The drafters of the Constitution, he concluded, "knew times can blind us to certain truths and later generations can see that laws once thought necessary and proper in fact serve only to oppress. As the Constitution endures, persons in every generation can invoke its principles in their own search for greater freedom."

So we must remember that the struggle for gay & lesbian rights has not been an entirely unsuccessful endeavor. At least in civilian courts, our sexual proclivities are no longer sending us to prison. It is, in fact, an entirely different era, some 110 years after the Oscar Wilde debacle. With new liberties and freedoms, in some respects we have arrived at an age of enlightenment – even if in other respects we seem to have gone backwards. In the nineteenth century, for example, there was a sort of homosexual renaissance in Europe, with periods of relative freedom in certain areas that extended into the early nineteen hundreds – only to fall back into a time of violent oppressiveness with the onset of World War II.

It is also helpful to consider the struggle and varied successes of other groups. The idea of equal treatment for blacks has made great strides in the past 50 years. One must remember that it wasn't that long ago when "separate but equal" was a codified legality. State-sponsored discrimination was the order of the day. We still have a long way to go before discrimination is a thing of the past, but we have come a remarkable distance in only fifty years.

Nor are groups immune from backlash. The abolition of slavery was too much success too fast for many Southern Christian Fundamentalists – the backlash resulting in the formation of the Ku Klux Klan. It is instructive to remember that, at it's height in the 1920s, a large number of Congressional representatives were members of the KKK. There has also been an irrational and sometimes violent backlash against innocent Muslims since the attack on the World Trade Center.

When it comes to personal liberties, all Americans have taken a hit since the attack on September 11, 2001. I recently received an email invitation to sign a human rights petition:

"Have you heard that George Bush is using the National Security Agency to conduct surveillance on American citizens without the consent of any court?

"This is specifically against the law. Bush says political appointees in the Justice Department outlined the legal authority to get around the restrictions in our laws and the Constitution, but those legal memos are classified.

"I just added my name to a formal Freedom of Information Act request to see these documents. We need to know if the president broke the law, and where this administration thinks the line of its authority is.

"You can sign on to the Freedom of Information Act request here:

http://www.democrats.org/page/petition/domesticspying/fduhyn

I did sign the petition but I also sent the following (tongue-in-cheek) response:

"Thanks for the informative email. I just added my name as well to the Freedom of Information petition, but was shocked to discover a suspicious looking van parked out front a few minutes later. I ignored it and lay down to take a nap, but was awakened by the sound of drilling, followed by a stream of bright light coming though a small hole in my bedroom wall.

"I rushed outside and the man assured me everything was OK, he was simply installing a small unobtrusive camera to monitor possible un-American activities. I started to get mad, but decided to comply after he informed me the wrong attitude could result in a flight to some undisclosed Afghani "hotel" with unusually harsh room service.

"Within several hours, they had installed hundreds of cameras around my house, and I ultimately decided, of my own free will, to remove my name from the Freedom of Information petition.

"I'd also like to take this opportunity to let everyone know I think George Bush is doing a fine job. He makes me proud to be an American."

So where does all this leave us? Better and worse, as the struggle continues. The way I see it, as long as the laws continue to change in favor of equal treatment for all, then personal discrimination should diminish. Moreover, I have resigned myself to the possibility that some pockets of anti-intellectual discrimination may never change.

But the small, still voice in me says things are better now than when I was younger. We can get married now in some states. It is no longer forbidden to talk about homosexuality, and more of us are "out" than at any point in history. That's what I would conservatively call major progress!

Do we need to proceed with caution? Sure. Is it ok to get angry from time to time -- does anger help facilitate change? Youbetcha. Will we see and end to the mind-numbing stupidity of hate and prejudice in our lifetime? The answer to that, I'm afraid, is a thundering "no."

The small, still voice tells me to keep up the good fight. The fate of humanity? Well that's up to a lot of other small, still voices. I am not, after all, my brother's keeper. I predict a favorable outcome if the world listens to its own small, still voice and if people come to understand that they are not their brother's (or sister's) keepers either.

Chapter 19: Health Care

I WISH I WERE a better communicator. I wish I could invent a turn of the pen, an inflexion of voice – a carefully selected string of words that would inspire in America a sincere quest for justice, a desire for fairness and equal treatment. But my thoughts flatten out on paper – the black ink inevitably fails to reflect passionate intent. The noble purpose gets lost in translation to the page before the ink has dried.

I have been thinking lately about health care – wondering why the United States has stubbornly refused to follow the rest of the civilized world in guaranteeing health care to its citizenry. I cannot, in fact, think of a single other first-world country whose citizens do not enjoy this guarantee.

Having always been a relatively healthy person, I guess I had never given the matter much thought. Now, however, the inadequacies seem apparent and glaring.

It is ironic that I have been spared a certain death sentence from the HIV virus (a complex illness successfully treated only at great expense), only to succumb to a simple kidney problem – all because health care in the United States is not a right, but a privilege guaranteed only to certain classes of people, such as the very wealthy and the very poor. It seems that fewer employees are offered health insurance every day. Many companies, such as Wal-Mart, evade their health care responsibilities by staffing primarily with part-time workers.

When I was in high school, I began to dream about buying my first car. I stopped by the Mazda dealership and picked up a brochure on the new RX-7 sports model. After practically memorizing the brochure, I began to notice RX-7s everywhere. I became an RX-7 recognition expert – I could spot one a half-mile away just by its shape.

The human brain works that way. We become "sensitized" to things and issues we're interested in, learning to recognize them when we see them. There weren't any more RX-7s on the road, but I had learned to see the ones that were there.

Similarly, once I learned the "ropes" of the hodge-podge health care network, I began to see how easy it was for people to fall though the substantial gaps in care. Such people have always been there, suffering for lack of care, but I only began to notice them after I became sensitized to look for them. Moreover, I find HIV patients at an unusually high level of risk because of the nature of "immune deficiency." Even when caregivers expertly treat HIV, they frequently are not allowed to treat the opportunistic illnesses that occur because of the HIV. And that's too bad, because no one ever died of HIV. When we die, it's always because of some opportunistic issue that happened while or because our immune system was depressed.

There is a large body of literature describing the enormous cost of "emergency room health insurance" being misused as the last line of defense for health care indigents. It seems to me the savings involved in eliminating the emergency room as a last resort for such people might go a long way in funding some kind of national health insurance. Just a thought.

In the meantime, I'll just wait. It's Sunday, September 3, 2006, over a month since Dr Borucki tried to arrange an emergency visit with a urologist for me, and I still haven't received the tests the urologist recommended because I have not successfully convinced the hospital of my ability to pay for the tests.

I see Dr Borucki again on Tuesday, my regularly scheduled visit for the pharmaceutical research program. They'll do blood work and take a urine specimen and I'm hoping the doctor might have some other kidney treatment ideas. Otherwise, I may not be eligible to receive care until it's too late to do any good. If this fact elicits sympathy, so be it. The point, however is simply that my circumstance has made me aware of some glaring inadequacies in our health care system. For my part, I have already been spared a gruesome death from far worse causes with far worse symptoms than my current kidney problems.

Part Three: Both, Taken Together

I have paid much for my beliefs. It must be my beliefs, since I have little sex to claim for my court martial or my AIDS.

It is one of the greatest ironies of my life, perhaps one of the greater ironies of our collective age, that any man should have exacted from him such a huge price for a life so unadorned by the comfort of human touch.

I'VE BEEN CONSIDERING THE CHANGE in my outlook between the first and second parts of this book. I find myself wondering why my former "dying" self chose to see beauty around me, whereas in my second incarnation I think more of the ongoing struggle for liberty and equality. I worry that this change in perspective might be seen as disingenuous. On one hand, issues of prejudice and intolerance were certainly present before; on the other hand, there is surely as much beauty around me now. So I ask myself why the change in focus.

Beauty and activism -- what's right and what's wrong -- are both important. They modulate each other and should be understood together to get a better idea of what's really going on. Having recognized the power of each separately, I now feel like exploring the synergy of both together. Why does the activist struggle if not to enjoy the beauty unfettered?

Chapter 20: Flowing Pen, a Story of Survival

I LOVED BEING A CREWMEMBER on C-130 cargo planes. It always struck me as a sexy aircraft, in the way some people think of classic motorcycles or cars. It has four big, noisy propellers that make it impossible to confuse with newer aircraft, but it also has a lot of power, giving one of the shortest takeoff rolls in the Air Force inventory. It can land in a dirt field, is just about indestructible, and is famous and beloved for getting its crews safely home. An airplane, like a ship, has a feminine gender, and in time takes on its own personality. Superstitions aside, it's more than a machine – it becomes one of the crew.

The C-130 has been around since 1954, making it one of the oldest airframes in the inventory. Like me, many of the planes I flew were born in the early 1960's, and they had the avionics to prove it. In modern days, I imagine C-130s are equipped with the latest in satellite positioning, but I remember when we didn't even use the then-predominant inertial navigation system, or INS. Instead, we used outdated and inaccurate radio navigation systems that required some finesse and the tempered experience of a seasoned professional. In other words, they required a navigator.

You enjoy a tremendous sense of accomplishment when you're such an integral member of a tightly knit crew. I am proud to be one of the last of a breed of professionals to use little more than a sextant to navigate across the Atlantic Ocean. I remember the excitement at finding myself exactly on course as we coasted in to Britain after a long, overcast flight. The crew counts on the navigator on such missions, and everyone ends up with a nickname. Mine was "Magellan."

I was in my late twenties, an instructor navigator, when I was called into my commander's office for a private meeting. "I've been watching you, Troy," he said "and I'd like to make you an offer."

The lieutenant colonel proceeded to tell me about "Flowing Pen," a top secret, presidentially-directed mission to Central America. The handpicked crews would base out of Howard Air Force Base in Panama for two weeks at a time, and then resume normal duties at Pope Air Force Base until called back for another two-week Flowing Pen mission. I told him that sounded fantastic to me, and within a month, I was sent on my first mission.

The Air Force serves three broad missions that require three types of aircraft. Tactical missions require fighter aircraft; strategic missions require bombers; and military airlift missions use cargo planes. Of the three, cargo is the only one that doesn't kill people (a bonus) and is therefore the only one that actually gets to perform its real mission during peacetime. In other words, cargo crews get to travel – double bonus.

Flowing Pen turned out to be an exception, however. Once we landed at Howard, two large roll-on skids were strapped firmly in place. The "skids" were actually self-contained "offices" full of high-tech listening stations that seated a dozen or so linguists and other experts we referred to as the "whiz kids" -- because we weren't supposed to talk to or even look at them. Even so, it wasn't too hard to figure out what we were doing. We were flying as close to some ground-based bad guys in Central America as we could in order to collect intelligence – simple as that.

The mission wasn't entirely without risk, either. Occasionally a C-130 would return to Howard after a twelve-hour mission to discover bullet holes in the wings or fuselage. While no one was hurt during my time in Flowing Pen, our risk was recognized by the Air Force. Ultimately, I would receive two coveted Air Medals for missions that put me in harm's way.

Our biggest risks, however, were not bad guys shooting at us but the act of trying to get off the ground. To explain why, I'm afraid I'll have to go into a bit of aviation science.

In order for an airplane to fly, it must have sufficient "lift" to get off the ground. Lift is affected by many variables, but primarily depends on three conditions in order to overcome the gravity that otherwise keeps us earthbound. Obviously, aircraft weight is a factor – the lighter the aircraft, the less lift required to get in the air. A second consideration is airflow. The more airflow across the wing surface, the more lift the wing will generate. When you're taking off, headwind is a good thing and tailwind is counterproductive (once airborne, the aircraft becomes part of the air mass, making headwind and tailwind far less important). The third consideration is temperature. Higher temperatures cause the air to be less dense, reducing the efficacy of lift as the air travels across the wing. Cold air makes takeoff easier. Hot air makes takeoff more problematic.

Having considered the science of getting airborne, let's turn our attention to the topography of the Howard runway environment. Panama is a mountainous country. Only fifty miles from shore to shore at the Canal, it is a thin strip of land with few locations suitable for runway construction. Howard Air Force Base was on the southern shore of the country, just across the canal from Panama City. The runway runs north to south – the south end pointing toward the Gulf of Panama, which in turn opens into the Pacific Ocean. On the other hand, terrain off to the north of the runway rises steeply toward the Cordillera Mountains – the "backbone" of the narrow land mass.

The terrain therefore requires takeoff and landing in opposite directions, which is quite unusual. To land, one must approach from the south, over the Gulf; and to take off, one must travel the opposite direction, *to* the south, avoiding the mountainous terrain to the north. The only problem with this setup is that the prevailing winds are also always from the north, forcing aircraft to take off with a tailwind, which is never the preferred direction, all things equal. Typically, this tailwind takeoff condition wasn't insurmountable, as long as the winds were light.

Panama doesn't enjoy changing seasons – at least not as residents of the continental U.S. experience seasons. Panama remains hot year-round, its periods divided simply into "rainy" and "not rainy."

So already, we had two enemies of lift working against us; a tailwind and hot air that lacked the preferred density.

The name of the game for the Flowing Pen mission was to maximize our "time over target," meaning we were tasked with remaining airborne as long as was technically feasible. This meant topping off the fuel tanks and taking off at the maximum gross weight. Prior to each mission, therefore, we did a lot of checking and double-checking of the complex equations that described the physics of takeoff. It was always a close call. Given the fluctuating tailwind, warm temperatures, and weight of the skids and fuel, we were stretching the C-130's theoretical ability to get into the air to its rational limits. I've flown enough miles to circumnavigate the earth many times, but Flowing Pen was the only mission I ever flew where we had to use a stopwatch to determine the "point of no return" on takeoff roll. The stopwatch was started on brake release, and the "time" represented our last chance to safely abort the takeoff, should we not have sufficient speed. Once "time" was called, we could not abort without rolling off the end of the runway – an unattractive option considering that our excess fuel could only serve to make for a larger fireball. The point-of-no-return timing inevitably came just a few seconds before we had sufficient speed to "rotate," or lift off the ground. For Flowing Pen missions, takeoff was always an unusually tense moment. In Air Force vernacular, the "pucker factor" was high.

On this particular morning, we had an early scheduled takeoff time of 0600 (6:00 a.m.). You start with the takeoff time, and back everything up from there. Thirty minutes prior for preflight, thirty minutes before that for mission planning, thirty minutes before that for breakfast. Then you figure in time for shower and transportation, ant it all added up to a 3:45 wakeup call.

We got to the plane just as the whiz kids arrived, completing our preflight as they settled into their cubicles in the cargo bay. When we got around to checking the radios, we called into the tower and asked for the wind conditions on the runway.

"Winds are 350[6] at 15, gusting to 25."

"Did you say gusting to 25 knots?" the pilot asked.

"Roger. 350 at 15 gusting to 25."

The pilot, a young 1st lieutenant, turned to the flight engineer. "Eng[7], how does that affect our takeoff roll?"

---

[6] 360 degrees is due north. 350 degrees would be, in seafaring terms, a "north, northwesterly wind."

[7] Short for "Flight Engineer."

"Well, it shoots us out of the ballpark, I'm afraid," the engineer answered. "15 knots of tailwind is our outside limit at this temperature. If we get a gust on takeoff roll, it'll knock us right out of the air."

The pilot looked nervous. "Are you sure?"

"It's not too complicated. Do you want to see the math?" the engineer responded.

I was the most experienced officer on board, and wasn't surprised when the pilot asked me, "What do you think, nav[8]?"

"I think its best not to argue with mother nature. She rarely loses a fight. Why don't we wait a few minutes and see what happens with the wind."

So we waited, checking in with the tower every ten minutes or so, but the answer was always the same. The winds whipping over the mountains continued to gust. Our set takeoff time came and went without us so much as taxiing out of parking. We began to talk amongst ourselves about the possibility we may have to abort the day's mission altogether.

Then a blue Air Force sedan pulled up in front of the aircraft. The base commander stepped out and motioned for the pilot to come down to speak. Considering the pilot's age and experience level, I went with him for moral support.

"You're supposed to be airborne, what are you doing?" he demanded.

---

[8] An Air Force colloquialism, "Nav" is short for "navigator."

"Sir, we cannot take off until the gusts die down.""

"Our engineers tell me there's no reason you can't take off now.""

"Sir," the pilot stammered "I trust my crew. If my engineer says it's not safe, I believe him.""

"Look, I was a pilot in Vietnam and we used to push the envelope all the time. There's plenty of cushion built into the math. Trust me – you'll be fine. Besides, if you go ahead with the mission, I won't have to call your boss back home and tell him you refused my direct order to take off.""

I couldn't believe my ears, but this asshole was trying to intimidate our young pilot into risking the lives of everyone on board – and for what? Howard was just the host base for the Flowing Pen mission; they weren't even part of our chain of command! As the base commander finished speaking, a security police vehicle pulled along side him and four SPs got out, as if he intended to have us arrested should we refuse to take off.

We retreated to the plane for a crew huddle, after which the pilot told the base commander we would not take off until the gusts subsided. The base commander sped off in a huff, but left the security police with us as an ongoing intimidator. I was proud of my young pilot for standing up for himself, but it was obvious he'd been shaken by the exchange, hoping he had done the right thing.

Fifteen minutes later, we called the tower and got the following response: "Winds are 355 (meaning still from the north) at 13 knots, gusting to... winds are 13 knots.""

Then I noticed the base commander's car was parked at the tower.

We started our engines and taxied to the north end of the runway. The security police car followed us and remained off to the side on the taxiway. Off in the distance, I noticed another security police car stop at the south end of the runway, on the perimeter road.

"This whole thing stinks like a setup," I said.

"Yeah, I know," the pilot answered, "but what are we supposed to do?"

"Tower, let's get one more wind check."

"Winds are 352 at 14 knots… and you are cleared for takeoff."

The pilot ran the engines to full power as we finished the pre-takeoff checklist. The plane surged forward as the brakes were released, and I started the refusal timing on my stopwatch. The pilots monitored the engines on the takeoff roll, while watching the airspeed indicator for sufficient rotation airflow.

"Time," I announced over the intercom, as the point of no return came and went and the end of the runway loomed ever closer. My heart raced as we rapidly chewed up more and more of the remaining pavement. Finally, with only 150 feet or so left, the copilot announced "rotate," and the aircraft lifted gently off the earth. Within a second, however, and at an altitude of only fifteen feet, something went horribly wrong. The aircraft canted ten degrees to the right and stalled, and everything went into slow motion.

I felt the jarring effect of landing as the tires slammed into the overrun, that safety area at the very end of the runaway painted with white stripes. The overrun serves little purpose aside from being decorative. I suppose it helps landing pilots visually confirm they're landing on a bona fide runway. I'm not even sure the overrun is stressed for the weight of an aircraft. Few aircrews ever get near the overrun.

I instantly, instinctively, knew what had happened. We had been hit by a gust of tailwind. I also instantly knew that touching down in the overrun at any angle would add drag at the moment we could least afford it – at a time when we were least likely to survive it. Looking out the windscreen, I saw the SP's car right in front of us, and we were on a collision course.

The struggling C-130 bounced off the runway, but the bounce had slowed us down. Now we had insufficient airspeed to climb. We were airborne again, but we knew that we couldn't survive a "bounce" off of anything else. At an altitude of five feet, we just skimmed over the top of the SP's car. The security policeman who had been sent there to intimidate us into taking off ducked to the floorboard of his car, sure we were going to take the top of his vehicle off. We couldn't have missed him by more than a few inches. I was close enough to see the terror in his eyes.

Soon, we were over the waters of the Gulf of Panama, but still we could not climb. Between the heat and our weight and being further slowed by our bounce in the overrun, we just didn't have enough "oomph" to escape the ground effect, which acts as a sort of atmospheric magnet very close to the ground. By the time we were two miles out, we had only climbed to 10 feet. At ten miles we were at fifty feet. By 20 miles, we should have been climbing through ten thousand feet, but we had barely reached a hundred. During this whole time, no one on the crew had said a word. No checklists had been completed, no communication with tower, nothing but absolute silence. That's because no one believed, until we got to a hundred feet, that we could have possibly survived what we had just survived.

"Happy birthday, everyone," I said over the intercom.

"Amen, brother," answered the pilot.

For at least two weeks after that, the whole world looked, smelled and tasted different to me, and it was better. Each new morning, I realized, was a gift. Nothing, aside from the subsequent Flowing Pen takeoffs, seemed very stressful. I had been shown a clear picture of how fragile are our lives, and felt thankful... as if I had been granted an entirely new second life. I felt privileged to be part of my own existence – part of an adventure story that had just been given a renewed franchise.

Since I was the author of my own adventure story, the experience inspired me to do something new with my life. I began reading books on the mechanics and theory of film. Within a short time, I had digested a whole library of books on film, from its humble beginnings to its profound influence internationally by Eisenstein, Gance, Ozu, Griffith, and other masters. Years later, this knowledge would help me bring insight to my students as I taught film classes at the Art Institute of Houston.

Odd how the survival experience affects different people at different times. When I was a child and was rescued from drowning by my father at a family campout, I was too young to understand what had almost happened. The experience left barely a blip on my radar screen. As I've grown older, however, I find it impossible not to look for deeper meaning in such experiences. A year ago, though I wasn't feeling well, I had no idea I had a terminal illness. Since then I've been diagnosed and came very near death. For a while, I struggled to understand what dying meant to me and those around me. Now, however, it becomes more and more clear each day that I have survived this experience, too. As I look back on my life, I realize I have been learning both how to live and how to die. With each "near miss," the idea of death becomes more commonplace – something to take in stride. "Death," in a strange way, has become part of my understanding of life.

The idea of living with death is not at all a morose preoccupation with dying, but rather a liberating realization that it is as natural and as tragic as breathing. Understanding that death is both not frightening and inevitable has liberated me to go for all the gusto I care to try.

I consider myself unusually blessed in the number and quality of people in my life I can call close friends. One friend, who was a fellow cadet at the Air Force Academy, now practices law in California. A quick internet search revealed to me the tremendous amount of volunteer work he does for the betterment of others. He serves on several non-profit boards in addition to maintaining a thriving practice. He has always been the most ethical person I know. But his life has been marred by the loss of his parents and the recent untimely death of a close friend. For years he has suffered from depression and thoughts of suicide to the point that he sometimes completely dissociates – shutting down his office and "disappearing," for a while, from the world.

Another friend was a fellow USAF navigator – my first housemate. He's a lieutenant colonel now, flying in Iraq, and is still as endearingly insane as ever. He is retiring soon, however, embittered by "pencil-pushing bureaucrats" who get in the way of operational matters. He became famous when, above the mid Atlantic, he tore up his charts and announced to a disrespectful copilot, "ok, you get us there." He taped his charts back together only after the copilot apologized for deviating from heading. After reading a few chapters of this book, he admonished me that it would be better if I removed all my liberal political references. Given his conservative perspective, we usually avoid talking about politics.

I met a third close friend at an artists' club in Fayetteville, NC. After years of struggling, she has only recently begun to enjoy the recognition of her talent she has always deserved. A rape survivor, she also battles depression and suicidal feelings – always falling back into the low self-esteem caused by brutal sexual objectification at the hands of her attackers.

Yet another friend was my business partner in an advertising business. His great talent and temperament was not diminished by a conniving ex-wife who left him just as he succeeded in making her own business successful. Now he is haunted by his physical distance from his daughter and an unspoken fear that he may never find the right woman with whom to share his life.

The last friend I have to tell you about was my housemate in North Carolina. He is a registered nurse with a big heart who helped me greatly as I grew more and more ill over the past few years. He also has a debilitating back injury that he worries will affect his ability to continue working and caring for his young daughter.

All these friends have several things in common, not the least of which is that they will always remain friends. We enjoy a bond undamaged by weeks or years apart. They are, without exception, each of them exceptional – whether due to their talents or the size of their hearts, they are the kind of friends you hang on to no matter what. Finally, each of these friends has been, in his or her own way, damaged, by life experiences.

I have a personal theory that likens the experience of being human to eating a cactus. We all take care to aim carefully for the sweet fruit found between and beneath the sharp spines. But try as we might, no one gets to eat without being painfully jabbed. We all end up with needles in our faces.

It seems to me that we are all "damaged goods," we have all suffered loss and debilitating grief as a result of being human. On the other hand, I can't think of a single person in my life whose warm and valued personality wasn't shaped, at least in part, by that very same sadness or loss. So, maybe our pain is an inevitable and necessary part of creating, from the raw clay of our personalities, the wonderful people we have become.

We're already aware of the fact that no one gets out of this life alive, but now I've discovered that we also must suffer. If suffering is the key to making us better people, then maybe we can learn to view suffering itself in a different light. Maybe we can use our personal hardships to become better people, and in that way, make the world a better place.

There were once two brothers who loved each other very much. They lived in a town torn by two violently opposed political factions. One side wanted a free city, but the other side, motivated by fear, insisted on the efficiency of a dictator who could act quickly and decisively to quash dangerous elements from within. As the debates continued, it became clear that there could be no reconciliation between the two political parties, so it was decided that the city would be split into two halves, with a wall dividing them. The north side was to be free, and the south side would be ruled by a dictator.

By the time the two brothers discovered these plans, it was almost too late to escape from the south side. They were deemed subversives, and the South Side Police had already issued a warrant for their arrest as they fled for their lives. As they neared the demarcation line, they could see that the wall was almost finished. The first brother easily cleared the wall, but as he turned to help the other over, saw he was being arrested.

"Go! Run… and be free," his brother yelled as the police dragged him into custody.

The brother on the north side wept as he watched his brother disappear into a police car and speed away….

Since then, the brother in the southern sector has been happy. He wakes in his cell each morning and is thankful that his northern brother is free. He sees his life as a gift, and lives in a world colored by his ability to imagine the freedom his northern brother must surely enjoy.

The northern brother rarely leaves his room. He carries with him the guilt that he should have done more – that he should have done something different or sooner. He thinks only of his brother, locked away in a cell, and cries himself to sleep every night.

Which brother is really free? If I am to live in a prison, I must realize it will be a prison of my own making. I have discovered that it is not the hardships in my life that contain me. On the contrary, these hardships have only served to make me stronger and better – more understanding, less judgmental. I am contained only by my own perspective, the attitude that says, "I can" or "I cannot." Between these two simple choices, our decision will determine the fate and extent of our ability to move and think freely.

Chapter 21: God, the Universe and Everything

This chapter is for my mom, who, having read my book thus far, felt there were a few things I needed to clear up.

CURRENT SCIENTIFIC THINKING has the universe starting this way: no one knows exactly what set off the Big Bang, but about thirteen billion years ago, everything we know of – the whole universe – was as small as an atom. Within a trillion trillionth of a second, an incomprehensibly enormous burst of energy was exploding in all directions.

That's how all this got started – as energy. Even the stuff we're mostly interested in, which is matter, started as pure energy. This makes sense in a weird sort of way, since when you look at the elements that make up our world on a small enough scale, they can all be described as various configurations of energy – certain combinations of electrons orbiting around certain combinations of protons and neutrons – all of them types of energy.

Within a fraction of a second, the explosion had already created hydrogen and helium – it took a little longer for other elements to form. Random collisions occurred as the explosion grew in size and as the energy from the original explosion began to decay.

Within that first second, scientists say, most matter was "eaten up" by near-equal quantities of antimatter – but for a singular anomaly, there would be no matter today. The anomaly is that for every hundred million particles of antimatter, there were a hundred million and one particles of matter. So everything we touch and can see in this massive universe is the result of that ever-so-slight tilt in favor of matter. Every atom in the universe had the odds of a hundred million to one not to exist at all.

Even then, a massive amount of matter had to survive in order to produce the infinite randomness required to bring about the varieties of collisions needed to create the diversity of elements we enjoy today. Over a hundred different elements, from oxygen to iron to carbon – all the elements that make up everything around us such as cars and computers and skyscrapers – were born in those first few moments as the universe began.

No one knows how long it took the universe to "invent" the complex amino acids that form the basis for all life, but even these are made up of those same elements – carbon, hydrogen, nitrogen oxygen – that were created by way of random collisions during the first few instants after the big bang.

The explosion created an incomprehensibly enormous flash of light. So enormous, in fact, that scientists say a full one half of one percent of all radio and television static you see even today is leftover radiation from that original bang all those billions of years ago.

Imagine the odds that this original bang could have created all the pieces that would someday lead to the creation of a being capable of reflecting on the very event that created it. In order to understand the miracle, I strike a match, and imagine a particle within the original explosion of flame expanding into a miniature universe that contains, in the instant just after its creation (and just before its extinction), a race of beings who, in the course of that instant, come close to understanding what they are – how they came about – how small they are.

I've purposefully left God out of the discussion to this point. Bear with me – I'll get back to God in a moment. For now, let's simply imagine we are random chance incarnate. Imagine that, as science indicates, we started as pure energy – gradually "colliding" into various forms of matter, and *voilà*, here we are.

Doesn't that make you feel rare? Doesn't it make you feel privileged – to be made up of particles that each had only one in a hundred million chances of survival in the first place? And then to be arranged in such a way as to exist and feel and think and love? If life wasn't already sacred enough, a solid understanding of how rare it is should instill in all of us a profound respect for the fact that there is any life, let alone ours!

I've only just begun to examine the beginning of the universe, and already I feel less inclined to kill or judge others – rather I feel like hugging and loving and just shaking everyone's hands and saying, "Congratulations – for we are indeed fortunate!"

And if, by chance, I can wrap my mind around the enormous diversity in the universe – that there are millions of types of collisions between particles that result in thousands of different types of reactions that form all these different elements and compounds and life forms and suns and planets and black holes and quarks… if I can even start to understand that, but for this diversity, we would not exist… why, then, do I stubbornly draw the line at homosexuality?

Which brings us back to God. Well, *my* God created nature, he or she doesn't rail against it. Imagine for a moment that God hadn't clearly instructed us to destroy all that is impure… imagine that God's instructions, rather than being printed in a book, were implicit in the diversity all around us – in the diversity of the universe, in the very energy and the elements all around us. Imagine that we can see God's will in the faces of all the people in the world – in all the variety of races around us. Imagine that God's will exists in the fact that a notable percentage of each species of animal[9] displays

---

[9] The famed National History Museum in Oslo, Norway, has been targeted by local church groups over a historic exhibit, "Against Nature," believed to be the first in the world to examine the role of same-sex animal pairs. A translation says: "We may have opinions on a lot of things, but one thing is clear -- homosexuality is found throughout the animal

homosexual tendencies, from flamingos to pigs to sheep to cats and dogs. Homosexuality is everywhere in nature! Was this really an error on God's part? Did God really not intend for such diversity to exist?

And exactly how does the concept that "homosexuality breeds homosexuality" work? The way I understand it, homosexuals don't breed at all. To my knowledge, a vast majority of *all* homosexual males and females were conceived by heterosexual parents.

But why must our sexuality be an issue in the first place? Is the very fact of our existence not enough for us to sit back in awe and wonder and mutual respect for all life... just for the enormity of the odds against it? Why can we not just smile and congratulate ourselves for making it this far? I have been given precious little time to love and exist and wonder... I hate getting bogged down in the mechanics of dealing with people whose "God" tells them I am an abomination and must be dealt with severely.

When I was very young, I was a sponge – absorbing information from all directions. Before I knew what sex was, I understood that I did not want to be a "homo" when I grew up. To be a "homo" was to be demented and perverted. No one wants that. So I fought those feelings. I denied them in myself and in the process denied myself my own childhood and adolescence. I continued denying them in my young adulthood. Not until I was thirty years old did I allow myself

---

kingdom; it is not against nature." Homosexuality has been observed in more than 1,500 animal species, and is well documented in 500 of them.

to consider the possibility that I might be gay, and even then, I proceeded with great trepidation – after all, who "wants" to be gay?

That's why I find it inconceivable that thinking humans could bring themselves to believe that being gay is a choice. Are there really, truly people out there who are stupid enough to think that someone wakes up one morning and decides, "hey, I think I'll live a persecuted life – I think I want to be ostracized by my friends and family – I think I want to be spit on by humanity – I think I don't want my seed to carry my gentle spirit through new generations – I think I'll choose to be gay." Even if you ignore the existence of homosexual behavior in other species, surely you can't think that anyone would choose to be gay. The fact that homosexuality exists in a society so hostile toward it is itself the greatest testament to the fact that it *cannot* be a choice. God has made his word manifest in nature itself – the instructions are clearly written in the world around us and within us. No one simply jotted down a few notes two thousand years ago with the intention that we should run with it. The instructions are alive, the Word is alive – and it's written everywhere you look.

And if we stubbornly insist on acting out violence against "sin" and "sinners," then let us do so without impunity. The twentieth chapter of Leviticus is where most of our rationale for killing gays comes from, so let's go ahead and implement the laws set forth.

"Anyone… who sacrifices his child as a burnt offering to Molech shall without fail be stoned by his peers." Apparently, this law doesn't apply if the child was sacrificed to a different god.

"I will set my face against anyone who consults mediums and wizards instead of me…" These are pretty strong words for those of us who occasionally consult the horoscope in the daily newspaper.

"Anyone who curses his father or mother shall surely be put to death…" This gives pretty clear instructions that we should not wait to let God judge the guilty party. We are instructed to put them to death now.

"If a man commits adultery with another man's wife, both the man and woman shall be put to death." Again, God makes clear that those people, like Jimmy Swaggart, who commit adultery, must be executed now.

"If a man sleeps with his father's wife, he has defiled what is his father's; both the man and the woman must die, for it is their own fault." Since the term "mother" is not used, I can't help but wonder whether the father in this case has remarried – which makes me wonder about biblical "family values." In either case, it seems a lot of people are being put to death for sexual misconduct. This law is also interesting because it explains its own rationale. The reason it is wrong for a man to sleep with his father's wife is because she is his "property." She is not here considered a person in the way a man is considered a person.

"And if a man has sexual intercourse with his daughter-in-law, both shall be executed; they have brought it upon themselves by defiling each other." It's curious that this law doesn't apply to a man's own daughter but only his daughter-in-law. Lot, you may recall, had intercourse with his own daughters – an act that was apparently allowed and (some would argue) even sanctified by God. From today's perspective, these are odd mores indeed.

"The penalty for homosexual acts is death to both parties." This is the first rule in the list that we hear from modern church leaders. Curious that we don't hear the death penalty being recommended for violations of the other laws.

"If a man has sexual intercourse with a woman and with her mother, it is a great evil. All three shall be burned alive to wipe out wickedness from among you." This seems to me to be an unlikely situation, though I'm not sure whether I follow the rationale behind what makes it a particularly criminal activity.

"If a man has sexual intercourse with an animal, he shall be executed and the animal killed." I just feel sorry for the poor animal. As if it wasn't bad enough the animal endured being raped, now it must also be murdered.

"If a woman has sexual intercourse with an animal, kill the woman and the animal…" In biblical times, woman were considered personal property, which is why the author felt the need to write a separate law that covered their behavior.

"If a man has sexual intercourse with his sister, whether the daughter of his father or of his mother, it is a shameful thing, and they shall be publicly cut off from the people of Israel." Once again, we see a biblical "nuclear" family, where the parents have remarried. It's curious to me that sex with your girlfriend's mother is punishable by death, yet sex with your sister will only get you ostracized.

"If a man has sexual intercourse with a woman during her period of menstruation, both shall be excommunicated, for he has uncovered her uncleanliness." Since menstruation was considered unnatural and unclean, the best thing for men was to avoid all contact with women during these "vile" periods.

"Sexual intercourse is outlawed between a man and his maiden aunt – whether the sister of his mother or of his father – for they are near of kin; they shall bear their guilt." For the first time in this list, no specific punishment is proscribed. So this is simply something you ought not to do.

"If a man has intercourse with his uncle's widow; their punishment is that they shall bear their sin and die childless." This is a curious law indeed. God here admonishes us that we should avoid our uncle's widow. I can't help but wonder whether followers are supposed to enforce the decree in the case where a child is born. Are good Christians supposed to then kill the children to ensure the widow dies childless?

"If a man marries his brother's widow, this is impurity; for he has taken what belongs to his brother, and they shall die childless." If his brother is dead, then how can he still "own" his wife? Nonetheless, we are clearly instructed that she belongs to her dead husband, and we are once again left with the question of whether or not God wants us to kill her children.

To be fair, many Christians recognize the coming of Christ as creating a new covenant between God and man that nullifies many of the rules set forth in the Old Testament. Nowhere is this example more poignant than Christ's nullification of our Old Testament requirement to sacrifice animals through the crucifixion. Christ himself was completely silent on the subject of homosexuality, choosing to talk more about ways we *should* behave rather than how we shouldn't. One notable exception is his repeated admonishments against divorce, which is interesting – since many of the most vocal religious critics of homosexuality are themselves divorced, yet they paradoxically remain fixated on the Old Testament rule sandwiched among all the other obsolete ones.

While Christ didn't say much about things we should not do, he spoke frequently about loving each other – to the point of even loving our enemies – and warned us against throwing stones unless we are without sin.

I go through this exercise to try to better understand God's will, and to try to figure out where all this hatred and violence and denial of civil liberties comes from. Try as I might, I find it difficult to reconcile this scripture with the current teachings of the church, and harder still to reconcile with my own sense of morality and justice, so I turn once again to the larger and more vibrant scripture – which is the legacy God left me in the form of the observable universe. All I need to know is written in the leaves of the trees and the sunlight and the love I feel and, yes, in the very randomness and diversity that makes all life possible in the first place.

I tune the channel on my radio to a place between the stations so I can listen to the static. Within the white noise, I hear the voice of God.

Chapter 22: My Confession

This chapter is dedicated to my brother, who deserves more than words.

I WAS A POOR EXAMPLE of an older brother. I was only a child myself, but looking back through the filter of more mature sensibilities, it's easy to see my own shortcomings. Being myself an unpopular child, I was too engrossed in finding my own place in the world to take the time to show my younger brother the affection he longed for and deserved. With only three years separating us, I often treated him as a cumbersome and even embarrassing "tag-along" in social situations. He would regularly be disregarded or asked to leave us alone as I attempted to make new friends my own age. I was far too engrossed in my own struggle for acceptance to be bothered with consideration for the younger brother who wanted only to be included in the enthralling activities of the "older kids."

Surprisingly, he always responded with love and affection, though he was often rebuked or left behind. As time went on, he would grow to idolize the older brother that never seemed to give him the time of day. Even when we were older and I began to regret the bond I had failed to nurture, I could not quite reach him. We remained separated by that distance I had created in our childhood.

For me the distance between us was held firmly in place by the guilt I carried for my neglectful treatment of him in childhood. For my brother, the same distance was maintained by the high regard in which he held me. He idolized me, which was both an inaccurate remembrance on his part and an incredibly unfair view of his own personhood – his own accomplishments and credit for the unqualified love he gave so freely.

I went on to graduate from the Air Force Academy and become an officer, while he got married and went into the Marines, serving in the Gulf War. He had a drug problem and a failed marriage, and I continued to receive the family's accolades and blessings. In some respects, I was the white sheep and he was the black sheep as we grew into our respective adulthoods.

He was profoundly upset over my court martial, and was first on the scene when I discovered I had AIDS. He continued to hold me on the pedestal he had carved for me in his imagination. I could not quite bring myself to accept the love he felt for the big brother who treated him so poorly in childhood. In my mind's eye, the image of his upturned five-year-old face saying "I love you, big brother" formed an indictment of an opportunity I had thrown away.

Then, yesterday, he called me from work to pick a fight. He told me that he was unhappy with the way I've been treating his five-year-old son, my nephew. He felt I'd been hard on him lately and made me promise, before he let me off the phone, to treat his son with more respect in the future. I was taken off guard and didn't know what to say, so I agreed and that was that.

But that wasn't *that*, after all. As the afternoon progressed, I grew more irritated. After all, I hadn't treated my nephew poorly, and therefore had nothing to apologize for. I grew more angry as I planned my rebuttal, which was to include an admonishment for not having had the courage to discuss the matter face-to-face.

I picked my brother up at 5 p.m. and didn't waste much time before lighting into him on the way home.

As adults, we rarely argue. I cannot, in fact, remember the last time my brother and I had an angry verbal exchange – so it became quickly evident as the shouting match progressed that our argument had little to do with my treatment of his son. It was rather the result of something deeper – some unspoken festering issue that had been boiling under the surface of the risk-free banter that defined our current relationship.

"Just tell me one thing," he said, as we rounded the corner on the final stretch of the drive home. "Did you really tell mom that you had no idea you could get AIDS by having unprotected sex? Do you really expect me to believe that the genius in the family was so stupid that he didn't realize how dangerous that was? Did you really tell her that?"

"Yeah," I said. "I just did it to piss you off."

"Just answer my question, please."

"That's not what I told mom," I answered.

I hadn't, in fact, told mom much of anything. I hadn't intended to tell anyone much of anything. I had convinced myself that the answer was extraneous to the story – a category of factual information that would only muddy one's understanding of what had happened and why.

We finished the drive in silence, but I had been shaken and startled by his question. I lay awake that night. The gravity of his inquiry gradually struck me with full force as I began to realize he had finally asked me the question he had never before dared to ask. The years instantly dissolved. I am once again eight years old and my brother five. Looking up, confused, he says, "You have outpaced me, brother. And now you have killed yourself. How will I ever catch up?"

The tears trickled onto my pillow, and I realized that I owed him the truth. The facts that before seemed secondary now became the central issue. I began to understand that what I owed to my brother, I also owed to my reader – it is precisely the thing that smashes the pedestal on which I have been placed – the high regard that separates me from my brother and the reason this book must be written. Far from being extraneous material, it becomes the crucial redeeming element – the thing that can perhaps finally close the distance that has separated us for so many years. I am not, after all, better than my brother. Let us, finally, greet each other on a level field, with mutual love and respect.

That was on Saturday, September 17. Early on Sunday morning, I hitched a ride with my brother to a location about five miles east of town – the home of a new friend I had met at my first local PFLAG (Parents, Family and Friends of Lesbians and Gays) meeting in Tyler on the previous Monday. Though it was a group of only ten, the local PFLAG chapter was the largest regular meeting of gays in Tyler, so I joined immediately. It just so happened that the annual Pride Parade, in Dallas, took place that day, and the East Texas chapter of P-FLAG had a float. I had arranged to ride with Terry, the float driver, in his pickup, towing the trailer that we would decorate as a "float" once we arrived in Dallas.

On the way to Terry's country estate, I nervously sipped my coffee – stealing glances of my brother's bleary-eyed profile from the corner of my eye. I knew what I had to say, but that didn't make the telling any easier. We had grown up together in Dodge City, Kansas, and both had ingrained in us a kind of familial relationship ethic that didn't allow for the explicit discussions of one's feelings. Our father loved us, but never said it in so many words. He expressed his love through his actions and through the gentle smile on his face. Our childhoods were enriched by many unspoken yet clear gestures of love from our father, and this had molded our own adult way of dealing with each other. Our credo, even now, is "Keep it short, get to the point, and don't be mushy about it."

I had already finished a cigarette... no more excuses for delay... so I set down my coffee and said, "It was drugs."

"You asked me how I could have been so stupid as to get AIDS," I continued, "I was high on cocaine – it affected my judgment. I've never told anyone about this, but when you asked me, I realized you have a right to know. There was nothing you could have done – it's not your fault." I started to choke up and he reached out... put a comforting hand on my knee. "I'm so sorry," I said. "You do something like that and you think it's only affecting you, but it affects a lot of people. I never meant to hurt you."

"It's ok, Troy," he said, and when he spoke, it was as an equal. The illusion of my "pedestal" – of my "superiority" – had revealed itself to be a trick of the light. We were, after all, on level ground.

He drove in silence for a few minutes, after which we picked up the conversation about driving directions. After a short while, we found Terry's house and he dropped me off. "I love you," I said before I got out of the car. "I love you, too," he answered.

East Texas is in the midst of what some experts are calling a ten-year-draught brought on by global warming. Most of my conversation with Terry on the freeway revolved around the stormy skies looming overhead. Rain has been so rare in these parts the past year that I wasn't too concerned about the chance it might rain on our parade. As it turned out, I was wrong.

We arrived safely in Dallas and quickly connected with other P-FLAG members. As we began decorating the P-FLAG trailer, the first drops of rain splashed on my head. I had never been to a gay pride parade before, and marveled at the professional floats all around us and throughout the staging area. We were right beside a big float for JR's (a popular downtown gay bar), whose riders frantically took up the task of placing sheets of plastic over enormous speakers and mixing equipment. They would soon be using these speakers to blast club music out to the audience.

All around us, plastic sheeting went up, covering the most sensitive paper and electronic parts of the beautiful floats. No one seemed to mind, however. The electricity of anticipation permeated the air like ozone after a lightning strike. Everywhere faces were smiling. The Texas Twisters rehearsed their dances without rain gear, their cowboy boots sending up great splashes of rainwater at each stomp.

I was agog at all this excitement. Even as the comparative inadequacy of our own float grew more evident, no one seemed to mind. We were here to celebrate diversity, and by God, nothing was going to stop us. To cheap green plastic table skirting, we tied dozens of hand-made paper flowers by means of pipe cleaners. The final touches included attaching two paper P-FLAG posters to the doors of the pickup. The posters had been lovingly constructed by gluing cut-out paper letters and a rainbow to a sheet of construction paper. By the time the parade started, the rain had already loosened one of the rainbows, half of which bent over under the weight. But it was all good.

Most of the P-FLAGers had chosen to walk, so it was just me and one of the moms riding on the float – on home-made upholstered benches that looked like they had been pulled out of a scraggly old camper. When we rounded the corner at the start of the parade, I was truly amazed at the size of the crowd that had gathered. Even though the rain was coming down in buckets, there were simply too many people present to imagine that anyone had stayed home – so many smiling faces and waving hands. As our "float" progressed, I was amazed by a wave of cheers that seemed to follow us. Our little float was getting a wonderful response. It didn't seem to matter that we were the tiniest, cheesiest float in the parade... everyone just loved P-FLAG. I found myself smiling almost apologetically, both for the humorously small size of our entry and for the fact that I was personally such a new member of P-FLAG – both points making me somewhat undeserving of the great warmth and love being showered on me.

At one point, I made eye contact with and waved to a young woman who seemed eager to get my attention. "I love your little redneck float," she screamed, humorously. This cracked me up.

"Thank you!" I answered, blowing her a kiss.

I was overwhelmed. So many friendly faces... so much love... so much potential for positive change... all of the onlookers oblivious to the pouring rain and the fact that we were all soaked to the bone. It was wonderful and it was miraculous and I was so happy I was part of it.

As I rode on our little "redneck float," I remembered an easily forgotten yet fundamental truth that applies to cities as much as to families. Love and respect, while both treasured and waterproof, don't cost a damned thing. There's plenty to go around for everyone.

Chapter 23: Silence Equals Death

THERE IS AN IMMINENT and overwhelming danger of presumption implicit within the bounds of silence. If we don't tell people we're gay, then we are presumed to be straight, which results in perpetuating the myth that our "gayness" needs to be hidden because it is dangerous – that *we* are ourselves dangerous. We are tired of various stereotypes – yet we still suffer these perceptions only where we have lacked the convictions to represent ourselves as ourselves.

Coming out is not simply good for us as individuals, it becomes a vital scream into the ether that we are the same people already known and loved by those who had presumed we were other than we are. The illusion of separation dissolves, and with it dissolves the presumption that we are dangerous entities that must be subdued or marginalized.

Similarly, my brother's plea for truth forces me to realize the importance of addressing the role of drugs in my life. Even after my personal revelations have been made and my own lessons learned, it is important for me to understand the intrinsic and obvious value of relating to others the dynamics of an altered state of consciousness in my life.

Cocaine did not simply cause in me giddiness that led me to be so cavalier with my own personal safety. Rather, it produced profoundly powerful urges and behavioral patterns that can only be described as self-destructive. It both facilitated carelessness and propelled it with great force. Even though I never intended to contract AIDS, the potential danger – the outside chance – seemed, under the influence of this powerful drug, itself an exciting thing. The fact that all this now seems so difficult to describe only serves to underscore the enormous power of the drug. It simply does not and cannot make sense, but the fact remains that I did not want or intend, or even imagine, that this single encounter would result in my illness. Even under the influence of the drug, the idea of getting AIDS was repugnant. Yet there I was, putting myself at risk, caught up in a moment of thrill.

And God knows, there have been few such moments in my life. The reason it is so easy for me to pinpoint the exact moment I contracted the AIDS virus is that I have had so few sexual encounters in my life. But my normal sensibilities did not save me from a single transgression. One lapse in judgment is all it took to transform the remainder of my life.

If it is ever possible to learn from the mistakes of others, I would pray that my revelation might perhaps save at least one other life. Avoid cocaine – it is more powerful than you are. And the news only gets worse as we learn there are many substances, such as crack and heroin and many others that make old-fashioned, powdered cocaine look like candy.

I write all of this knowing that many people must learn such lessons for themselves. If only I knew the right words to communicate the dangers involved in drugs that turn one's values upside down and inside out. Even today, more than a year since my last taste of cocaine, I still crave it.

I wouldn't be so bothered by all this if it just affected me, but this is not the case. I have created a burden for my friends and my family and even the society I was so interested in bettering. Is my legacy, after all the tallies are in, a negative number? I hope not.

We know that many drugs, such as alcohol, marijuana and nicotine simply aren't good for you. There is, however, a quantum difference in my opinion between these common intoxicants and cocaine, methamphetamines and heroin, among others. While everyone reacts to these drugs in a variety of ways, the hard-core varieties are more likely to bring about profound behavioral shifts. In my case, my inhibitions were sufficiently lowered to cause me to put myself at risk – but the actual experience makes it feel like an insufficient explanation. My experience was more like a strong inclination to act in ways so self-destructive and contradictory, I find them impossible to reconcile with a sober mind.

The message I would hope to convey is that drugs can make you into a person you don't like, and one who doesn't have your own best interest in mind. It only takes a single mistake to change your life or even end it.

As if the risk of getting AIDS weren't sufficient, there was a new participant at my group counseling session yesterday who made me aware of another reason to stay away from drugs. A struggling mother of two who contracted HIV through intravenous drug use, she has discovered that much of the aid she would have otherwise been eligible for is simply not available to people with drug convictions. The prevailing political attitude toward people with drug convictions is quite hostile, in fact, and tends to make getting any kind of assistance difficult or impossible.

My confession regarding the role of drugs in my illness has no personal cathartic value for me, and I certainly don't share this part of my story for the purpose of making myself look superior or more heroic – since my disclosure of drug use has the opposite effect. There's only one reason, and I have my brother's poignant question to thank for making me aware of it: silence equals death. I must be honest *especially* when it hurts; since that's the only time being honest truly matters. As I became more active in the local gay community, mom expressed some concern for my safety. While recognizing the potential hazards, I feel that it is far more dangerous not to speak out, because, again, silence equals death. I share my story in the hope that it will help someone heal or live or grow or learn.

Today is Thursday, September 21, 2006 – my 45th birthday. To celebrate, I have forgone my family's invitation to go out to dinner. Instead, I'm going to a training session tonight at Tyler AIDS Services in preparation for my volunteer work next week at the AIDS information booth at the state fair. In only two weeks, I've joined P-FLAG, been to my first pride parade, started designing a program for an upcoming AIDS benefit and will have volunteered at the state fair. For the first time since moving here, I feel connected with my community. I feel alive and I feel fortunate to be alive. How cool is that?!

Chapter 24: Kidney Pie

When life hands you kidneys, make kidney pie.

MY CREATININE[10] levels had risen to 2.1mg/dl, alerting my doctor of a potentially serious strain on my kidneys. His concern was that, left unchecked, the added stress on my kidneys might result in the need for dialysis or transplant. Unfortunately, there is no provision within the various AIDS and other health care programs

---

[10] From www.medicinenet.com: Creatinine is a chemical waste molecule that is generated from muscle metabolism. The kidneys maintain the blood creatinine in a normal range. Abnormally high levels of creatinine thus warn of possible malfunction or failure of the kidneys, sometimes even before a patient reports any symptoms. It is for this reason that standard blood and urine tests routinely check the amount of creatinine in the blood. Normal levels of creatinine in the blood are approximately 0.6 to 1.2 milligrams (mg) per deciliter (dl) in adult males and 0.5 to 1.1 milligrams per deciliter in adult females.

for preventative kidney treatment. All the local, state and federal programs have strict guidelines that require the patient to wait until after their kidneys fail before receiving assistance.

The health care system was failing me. After my initial visit to the hospital, arranged by Dr. Borucki, the receptionist called me one day with the new that she was not allowed to schedule testing or a follow-up visit. She gave no reason. When I called her the following week, she said she *was* able to get me an appointment – but I'd have to come in ahead of time to discuss payment arrangements.

Several days later, I sat down at a desk with a customer service representative who explained to me that the cash price for the kidney ultrasound I needed was $363.60, but that I could also take up to a year to pay, assuming I could put at least 25% down on the day of the test. Some quick mental math produced a figure of less than $100 down and about $25 per month, but she quickly explained that's not how it worked. The hospital had a completely different pricing schedule for patients who pay over time. In my case, the price for an ultrasound increased to $606, which included, presumably, $242.40 interest on the principal of $363.60, or 67%, which is three times the amount of interest allowed by law.

The hospital gets around the law, however with a few clever semantic tricks. The ultrasound price that includes interest – the $606 price – is called "the price," and the cash price – the $363.60 price – is called the "cash discount price." The hospital thus avoids the murky topic of interest and various legalities associated with payment plans.

Forgive me… I'm just a simple country boy… but where I come from, the "cash" price is just called "the price." Everything else is interest. I think the hospital knows they're on shaky legal ground on this topic. They got nervous when I asked for printouts of the two payment options, saying, "We don't do printouts here."

The customer service lady asked me whether I understood my options.

"Yes," I said, "but I'm not sure if I understand why you charge poor people almost double what everyone else has to pay."

"Aw, c'mon…" she said, laughing off my remark as if I had been joking.

The charge for the ultrasound was relatively small, though it was obvious to me that – depending on the results of this initial testing – I would be in no position to make similar arrangements for surgery or more expensive testing. Should the bill, for example, be in the $20,000 range, I would not have the resources to pay in cash, let alone the 67% higher price for paying over time. Without sufficient funds to pay the hospital's minimum of 25% of the 67% higher price prior to receiving care, I would simply be turned away.

While I was making arrangements for an ultrasound, Dr. Borucki's was making a few additional calls on my behalf. Thanks to his help, I was able to see a urologist a week after my ultrasound. Dr. Borucki's appeal on my behalf had also reduced my up-front and out-of-pocket expense to a mere $60, which is truly miraculous, given the variety of testing the urologist administered. I received another ultrasound, a prostate exam, and a test where a camera was passed through my urethra to view the condition of my bladder.

The urologist, a strikingly young, yet comfortingly competent, "Doogie Howser" type, digested the various test results and informed me that surgery or other procedures would likely be necessary, but that neither I nor my kidneys were in immediate danger. In other words, he believed it would be safe for me to wait the remaining year and a half, when Medicare kicks in, before seeking treatment. He scheduled a follow-up appointment six months later, and I left the hospital in a remarkably good mood.

Much of the issue with my kidneys revolved around fear – the fear of not knowing and the fear of not being able to find out. For the first time since being diagnosed with AIDS ten months ago, I found myself in the uncomfortable position of being told I could not get testing or treatment – and the old familiar fear, when I was laughed at in the North Carolina Social Security office, immediately resurfaced. This is the fear of being told that my "case" doesn't merit assistance. My sense of security apparently remains fragile – I remain sensitive to issues involving the metering out of care and who is and who is not deemed worthy of help. In many respects, the "system" is so fractured and hodge-podge that it's a wonder anyone gets anything done.

As it turns out, I've been lucky time after time – lucky for the great AIDS assistance programs in East Texas, lucky to get into a pharmaceutical research program, and lucky to be assigned to Dr.

Borucki, who has gone the extra mile to make sure my luck has held out through this "kidney issue."

My discussion of hospital pricing should therefore in no way be construed as an ungrateful assault on a health care system that has, after all, been kind to me. I point out the inequities only for the purpose of pointing them out. It is my hope that drawing attention to such issues can itself be an instrument of change, and thereby help others

My recovery is complete. The one remaining shadow has, at length, been dispelled. During my drive home from the hospital I found myself singing out loud. It feels good to feel good.

Chapter 25: Love and Sex

TODAY IS TUESDAY, SEPTEMBER 26, 2006, the last day of my volunteer work at the AIDS information booth at the Tyler annual fair. Before going to the fair, I'll drop off the mock-up program I designed for an AIDS benefit dance coming up in October. I've chosen a 1930s retro style that I've put quite a lot of thought and work into. I hope they like it.

The blues bar I owned and managed in Wilmington is still in operation. When I left town, my two non-managing partners had to rise to the occasion, and by all accounts, they've done a great job. The bar's relationship with the local blues society remains strong, and I wish them the best. Opened in 1957, the Rusty Nail is one of the oldest bars in town. May it enjoy many more years as a business where all people are welcome.

I've learned the cathartic value of keeping a journal, and intend to keep writing long after my current adventure is a distant memory. Moreover, I recommend the practice – jotting down every few days whatever may be on your mind. It's a good way to keep your sanity, or in my case to minimize my insanity.

I believe in activism, and intend to continue and expand my local volunteer work with both gay and HIV organizations. I picked up a bracelet made of rainbow-colored chain mail at the Pride Parade in Dallas a few weeks ago, and I've been greatly enjoying wearing it around conservative Tyler. It may not sound like much, but you'd be surprised what raises eyebrows here.

Speaking of Dallas, I'd almost forgotten what an incredible town it is. I've already started dreaming of moving there someday, though I'm torn between staying where activism is most needed or moving to a much more gay-friendly Dallas.

My symptoms, aside from occasional kidney soreness, are almost completely gone, with one exception. I still have unusually vivid dreams, presumably a side effect of my HIV medications. I typically get up once or twice each night to ponder tales that can be as realistic as they are fantastic. This is easy to live with, however. And who knows, it may even be helping my creative process. In any case, I feel good enough that I spend most of my time these days thinking of issues outside of myself – and any doctor will tell you that's a good indication the patient has recovered.

Some readers have asked me about Daniel, the guy I mentioned in Chapter 5 as the "love of my life." Daniel and I were in a committed and monogamous relationship that began quietly even as my court-martial was underway in 1992. We remained together for nearly nine years, breaking up during a rough patch and for no particular reason.

My libido remains at a low ebb – and given the delicate condition of my kidneys, my doctor is hesitant to put me back on male-hormone therapy. I therefore don't spend much time these days thinking about sex or personal relationships, whether long- or short-term.

Update

Fast forward to late February of 2008. The first edition of this book has been out for about a year, and I'm now doing my first major revision, with the help of a couple of dear friends.

I was sitting up last night with my friend, Tom, who asked me about my love life. Not as in, "How's your love life?" But as in, "Tell me how you have come to this place in your life and in love."

Since parts of my book were being re-written, here was an opportunity to clear up a point or part of the history of my life that needed clearing up.

He didn't understand… my editor didn't understand, and other friends were having trouble with my leaving out from my life story any substantial information about my relationships… my "love life."

I tried to explain about my nine-year relationship with Daniel, how he had been a saint to have put up with what amounted to a frigid partner for so many years, and how I couldn't blame him for finally giving up on me and leaving. Then I told him about Lance, whom I met just a few years ago…. And how, at age forty-one, a twenty-year-old kid took me under his wings, and I discovered sexual ecstasy for the first time in my life. The relationship with Lance lasted only six months, but it was for me my first true love story – the kind of passionate romance I used to think only existed in books and movies.

"It doesn't make any sense," Tom replied. "Don't you see, Troy, your story is backwards. Once you survived the court-martial, you should have been free to pursue the love of your life. But instead you went into a long relationship where you say you were 'frigid,' only to stumble across this short romance in your forties? How can this be?"

I sat there, squirming under the weight of his question, my face flushed with embarrassment. It was the same old feeling I always had when I tried to explain my life story to other people. Suddenly, I felt alien. Maybe I had less in common with "normal" people than I had wanted to believe....

For me, the succession of events from which my life was made seemed obvious. "C" follows "B," which in turn was of course preceded by "A." Furthermore, it's harder to explain the story when my audience is having trouble believing me – and in any case, it's tougher to talk about, realizing that so few people can relate to my experience. Lastly, it was a difficult experience for me the first time around, so remembering it wasn't going to be easy, either.

I was raised in a very conservative, charismatic church. When I was a kid, the Assembly of God preacher and Sunday school teacher taught me that dancing and movies were inherently evil. We didn't dare discuss anything as horrific as homosexuality. I didn't dare think about it, and passed off my urges as (please oh please, God) a temporary phase.

So I really did grow up thinking that gay sex was too dirty to even think about. When I couldn't stop thinking about it, I felt dirty, ugly, guilty and unworthy – which, I suppose, caused me to strive harder to overcome my "unworthiness." Maybe that's how I ended up at the Air Force Academy and became an instructor navigator, and how it could be that I didn't even start to take ownership of my gayness for such a long time. In other words, my guilt and fear is why I didn't come out, even to myself, until I was thirty years old.

And all of this by means of saying that I was already pretty messed up when I was court-martialed. I had just barely made an initial attempt to believe that being gay was OK, when the full weight of the U.S. government came crashing down on me, saying, "You are not OK, you are a criminal, and should be put in prison." If I was already frigid – just beginning to think about exploring gay sex -- then how could all the ensuing national publicity and public humiliation liberate me?

Being court-martialed did liberate me in many important ways. From that point onwards, I would live openly and proudly as a gay man. Eventually, I would regain my sense of humor and my self-confidence. Yet for many years afterwards, I would agonize over sex, because sex had been once again made evil for me… Intellectually, I knew sex was OK, that it was good and right. But on a deep level, I was afraid of sex. I was helpless against the fact that it seemed wrong to me. Some rape victims experience a similar effect, which may be a type of post traumatic stress. All I knew was that I hated sex, and the more pressure I or others put on me to perform sexually, the farther I receded into the safety of my subconscious self-loathing. This is the main tragedy and irony of my life – that I was traumatized so harshly for doing something I was emotionally incapable of doing in the first place – which in turn made me even less capable of doing it.

This brings me back to Daniel – Daniel, who decided upon seeing me across a crowded dance floor that we were meant for each other. He approached me just before my court martial, and we started dating. Looking back, it's very funny to think that I went on my very first gay date (an entirely innocent dinner-date) in the midst of a court martial that accused me of having been a long-standing and prolific gay dater and sodomite. In retrospect, I guess that took some balls!

We went on several dates just as stories about my upcoming court martial began to hit the local press. The story hadn't gone national yet, but it wasn't long before it was an almost daily affair to see an article about me on the front page of the Fayetteville, North Carolina newspaper. To avoid suspicion, we'd therefore usually drive to Charlotte for our evenings out. I think it was all exciting for Daniel to be dating someone in the public eye, but it also took a lot of courage on his part, and I respected him for it. From my perspective, he was an enormous comfort who came into my life at the exact moment when my life was crumbling around me. He held me up. In those days, he gave me strength to face the scrutiny of each searing sunrise.

I did my best to explain to Daniel that I wasn't emotionally capable of having sex – at least not yet -- but he was persistent. For his part, he promised that it wouldn't matter – that he would work with me for as long as it took. He was willing to be my partner, even if our relationship stayed platonic indefinitely.

For my part, I found his proposal irresistible. I couldn't imagine ever meeting another guy who would promise to "have and to hold me" without ever demanding sex. I also hoped that, in time, I might learn to enjoy sex – that I might be able to someday overcome the trauma that had been so painfully branded into my brain.

I had met a guy a few months prior to meeting Daniel who was raised not far from Fayetteville, and who, at 24, still lived with his parents. While he was still a minor, his folks had sent him off to some religious "gay conversion" facility, where they actually hooked electrodes to his testicles and shocked him while showing pictures of naked men. This procedure proved to be totally ineffective. Aside from being emotionally traumatized, he was still a gay man who enjoyed gay sex. At the time, I remember feeling sorry for him, and considered his treatment barbaric. I had no way of knowing that a few short months later, my own court martial would be far more successful than electrodes in putting me off of gay sex!

Eight and a half years after we made our commitments to each other – eight and a half years after my court martial -- sweet Daniel got tired of waiting. Losing him broke my heart, but it was probably best for both of us. We had come to a place where neither of us was happy. Just as he had been the one with enough courage to date a guy in the midst of a court martial, he was also the one with enough courage to end it when the time had come to end it.

It was 2001. I was a new bar owner, and was busy with booking blues and jazz bands into the Rusty Nail. Within one year, I would contract AIDS after sleeping with a friend. But I didn't know that yet. Nor did I know that I was about to learn to enjoy sex for the first time in my life.

Lance was beautiful in every respect. From his short sandy hair, to his olive complexion, to his handsome, twenty-year-old face, to his slender build, to his understanding of literature and poetry, to his ebullient personality – he was just perfect to me in every way. I didn't realize he was only twenty when he sat down at the bar.

I thought he was twenty-one, because he told me he was twenty-one.

He told me he was twenty-one because he wanted to meet me, and he was supposed to be twenty-one to sit in the bar.

He wanted to meet me, because the whole thing was a set-up. A mutual friend had decided that we "simply must meet."

Our mutual friend had been simply right!

Lance and I got along right away. Within minutes, we were cracking each other up, joking about our apparent blind date. He was so gorgeous that I couldn't believe I was talking to him — but more than that, he was smart, funny, and he seemed to be completely absorbed by me! For the first time since I was a kid, my heart was racing with a high-school crush... I was smitten.

Six months of adventure followed -- six months of absolute joy. It didn't matter what we were doing. As long as we were together, we were in heaven. Often, I'd spend the night at his apartment. Often, we made love. There was no dominant or passive between us. We melded into a single human being. Touching his skin made me feel wonderful, and holding him in my arms was paradise. Before meeting him, I could not enjoy sex, let alone be able to write about it.

All of the debilitating fear and guilt melted away when I was with Lance. For the first time in my life, I didn't feel that I was expected to perform or that I might let someone down if I didn't... I simply felt passion and love and tenderness and passion. Yes. I know I said "passion" twice.

Who's to say what might have happened if we hadn't broken up? I most likely wouldn't have AIDS, for one thing. But you know what they say about hindsight. The fact was that he was twenty (twenty-one by the time we split up) and I was twice his age. As much as I loved being with him, the "we" had always felt like a fantasy to me. As grateful as I was, and as joyous had been our time together, I couldn't quite solidify the image of a long-term relationship with someone who had been eleven at the time of my court martial.

But I owe a lot to Lance, my sweet, dear Lance, who taught me how to not be afraid.

After I wrapped up the telling of my story, my friend Tom looked at me and smiled. "Earlier in your book you called Daniel the love of your life. Maybe it was Lance, after all."

I thought about this for a moment, and replied, "Maybe you're right, Tom. Maybe it was both of them."

Chapter 26: Friendship

TODAY IS OCTOBER 12, 2006 – 5:45 in the morning. I'm sipping coffee while a hundred thoughts flood through my head – thinking about how ridiculous it was for me to let my feelings get hurt yesterday when I wasn't eligible for housing assistance. All because I was living with people I'm related to… while I would have been eligible for help with my rent if there were no blood ties with my landlord. I've been way too fortunate to get upset over something as trivial as that.

My brother and I were sitting on the back porch, enjoying the perfect seventy-two degree weather yesterday when he asked me rhetorically why it's so much harder to make good friends the older you get. We're both transplants to this Texas town and have both felt the isolation of moving to a new place as older men than we were in previous moves.

It is curious – the older people get, the harder it becomes to develop the close bonds necessary to define friendship. Stephen King wrote a poignant short story entitled "The Body," which was made into a superb movie called "Stand By Me," which was about the tender and innocently intimate bonds we easily form at age thirteen. Curious that within a few years that level of friendship becomes nearly impossible to re-create – a level of intimacy that continues to decline throughout one's life until, at my age, one is considered lucky to achieve the level of "casual acquaintance" in newly-formed relationships.

It seems a tragic result of aging that we are no longer willing to invest the energy required to nurture truly close friendships. It's easy enough to maintain the old ones, but we become less willing, over time, to invest in new persons of interest in our lives.

But those thirteen-year-old buddies did require a lot of energy. In them, we invested the telling of our dreams and our plans and the secret sharing of our childhood affections. They were both the source of and a test audience for our new jokes; and only they knew our most secret fears and insecurities. They knew us like no one had ever known us – like no one could ever know us again. Lucky are those who still have connections with friends they have known since that tender age… I have none.

At least as intense as the amount of energy invested was the level of pain involved when those friendships came to an end – when dad was transferred and we had to move to a different small town in Kansas, all those friends just faded into memory, and it hurt. Then, I thought I would never ever meet friends as good as the ones I lost. And I was right. Partly because I grew less likely to invest so much in new friendships that I now knew could not be permanent – and partly because it hurt too much to lose them – my friendships gradually shrank to become something less than they had been when I was thirteen years old.

Tomorrow, I'm driving mom up to Sterling, Kansas to see my 102-year-old grandmother. She's always been especially beloved to me. Her untiring spirit and positive outlook have helped me to stay centered through more than a few crises. She was a young woman during the Roaring Twenties, and was already considered "middle-aged" by the Great Depression. What wonders she has seen, what a life to have lived!

She was just put into hospice care. We're driving to Kansas to say goodbye.

My grandmother has always enjoyed remarkably good health and has always been loathe to make the smallest complaint, though I have noticed a change in her recently. She began feeling isolated – the inevitable yet somehow startling result of outliving one's peers. Then, in the past few weeks, the isolation extended to her senses: she has been unable to hear, to walk, to read even large text. She is cut off from the outside world. I think that would be a frustrating thing at best; at worst it would be utterly terrifying.

Some people believe that there is a river of energy in the cosmos that rains gently upon the earth, the droplets collecting in pools that we call "souls." When we die, they say, the droplets float upward to rejoin the river. While parts of this theory are comforting – even compelling – I prefer to believe that our souls remain discrete. I would rather think that our personalities transcend death than believe they simply merge into a grand continuum of souls, losing their distinctness in the process. If my soul is a glass of water, I find it more comforting to belive it might remain a glass of water, even after being poured back into the ocean of souls.

My hope stems less, I suppose, from a desire to keep myself intact, and more from a wish that I will be able in the afterlife to retain ties to the marvelous friends I have found in this life. I would like to think that I may meet my grandmother again – and my loves and my friends and my family. These are valued and engaging people, and I think it would be a shame if it turns out the cosmos had made no provisions for keeping their souls intact for all time.

Rather than lamenting and worrying over things I cannot change, however, I have resolved to focus on things I can – things like making friends. Just because it may be harder to foster and nurture new friendships than it has ever been, doesn't mean it can't be done. I have found many wonderful people, but I'm sure there are still a few out there. It's a little like mining for gold. You just have to look in the right spot.

Now it's October 20, 2006. Grandmother rallied when we arrived, and she intends to stick around awhile, which is fine with me.

Even at 102, she still seems in charge of her own destiny, which I find comforting.

I've come a long way, from terrifying hallucinations to my present sense that I'm not much the worse for wear. Tomorrow is Saturday. My six-year-old nephew has a soccer game in the morning. Those kids are so cute out there on the field, easily distracted but still managing to score goals while secretly building the self-confidence that will hold them in good stead for the remainder of their lives. I'm so proud of him.

At his last game, he reached up and touched the brightly colored rainbow bracelet I wear on my wrist. "What's that, Uncle Troy?" he asked. I just smiled and said, "That's for luck." He's having way too much fun being a kid right now – there will be plenty of time for politics when he's a little older.

Saturday afternoon I'm scheduled to participate in one of the MENSA national testing days to see whether I'm smart enough to join. The thought of joining MENSA produces on my face an involuntary self-deprecating smile, since I always thought they were a bunch of elitists, anyway. But then it occurred to me that I might find some friends and even kindred spirits there. I guess I was hoping I might find some people who were willing to think for themselves and draw their own conclusions.

There was an article in *The Advocate* about Kyle Rice, a gay fundamentalist Christian who is undergoing "ex-gay" therapy to try to become straight. I wish him the very best, but the topic reminds me just how unthinking fundamentalists can be. We all know that our children grow up smarter when we tell them they are smart… they grow up well-adjusted when they are surrounded by a loving environment… so why do some Christians believe their children will be anything but suicidal when they grow up hearing that they are fundamentally wrong and evil? The whole viewpoint that we must change what we cannot change only serves to make us feel valueless and leads, in my opinion, to the disproportionately high suicide rate among gay youth. If only these fundamentalists would think about their children before they try to convince them that an unalterable part of their personage must be altered because it is inherently wrong. It's like telling your child she will never get into heaven with red hair. She can color it, of course, but she will always know she is naturally red-headed and therefore unworthy. There are few things we can do to children so preposterously damaging as the mantra imposed by fundamentalists that there is something wrong with their gay and lesbian selves.

Chapter 27: The Remainder of My Life

IN 1979, when I was a seventeen-year old high school senior, I was approached in the hall by two popular cheerleaders who asked me to sign a petition to ban homosexuals from teaching in public schools. They felt the rationale for such a policy was so self-evident that no further explanation was needed. Their petition had a small paragraph at the top, and was already covered with student signatures.

Without thinking, I laid into them. "What are you doing?" I said. "If this is successful, you'll be sending American civil liberties a hundred years backwards."

I was immediately embarrassed and walked away without waiting for their response. Even then, part of me knew that I was gay, and I feared I had just outed myself, which, in 1979 for a high school senior, was the worst thing I could imagine. If you had told me then that I would later be publicly humiliated in a nationally publicized court-martial for being gay, I very likely would have committed suicide. There was simply nothing I could imagine that could possibly be worse than being a "homo."

That same year, I found myself daydreaming in Mr. Polk's civics class. I suddenly experienced a revelatory moment and began furiously scribbling notes about a concept for a new society. The idea revolved around an egalitarian commune that might grow eventually to replace our American culture of fear, violence and prejudice. My commune was self-governing; abolished currency, replacing it with work-credits; and treated all its citizens with equal love and respect. Fundamental to the idea was that, placed in a nurturing environment, people were basically good and crime could not flourish. Separated from corrupt cultures, new generations would make enormous advances, both spiritually and technologically, unfettered by the constraining influences of hatred and violence.

Within a few weeks, I had an entire notebook filled with ideas on how my Utopia would work, and I decided to devote my life to seeing it realized.

I began to research the topic, and ran across a book by the famous behaviorist B.F. Skinner called *Walden Two*. Ostensibly a novel, the book actually introduced the reader to Skinner's behaviorist theory and created a world in which there was no money or crime or hatred or violence. His plan was, in fact, virtually identical to the one I had been outlining and this was tremendously exciting to me.

The late 1970s were exciting years for many reasons, not the least of which was the fact that America had conquered space. Carl Sagan and others published book after book on the potential of space and space colonies. The new Omni magazine and Popular Science made living in space seem imminent and inevitable. We seemed on the verge of true, great and expansive progress. Anything was possible.

For me, space seemed like the obvious place to try my new ideas for an experimental society. For the experiment to work, I new that it had to be completely separated from the corrupting influences of the existing world. To my youthful sensibilities, behaviorism and technology had come together to create a unique moment in human history – an opportunity to achieve in the technology of human development advances that would rival those we had achieved in space technology.

All this was so exciting that I immediately applied to the Air Force Academy. My plan was to become an astronaut and work, as a behaviorist, on the first space colony, realizing in the process my (and Skinner's) dream.

Once I was accepted to the academy, I actually wrote Skinner a long, heartfelt letter, disclosing to him his great inspiration to me and my plans to help him realize his experiment. He actually wrote back to me, and we exchanged, for a while, letters that I still treasure today.

But *Walden Two* had been published in 1948. By the time we began exchanging letters, Skinner was an aging professor emeritus at Harvard, and even he held out little hope that his ideas would be completely successful in eliminating crime, hatred and prejudice. As the 1980s progressed, and maturity tempered my youthful exuberance, the idea of being a space pioneer-cum-behaviorist world-builder receded into the realm of science fiction. Moreover, the idea that the world could ever be perfect proved to be as undesirable as it was unattainable.

It would be a mistake, however, to say this experience is the reason I graduated from the Air Force Academy with a degree in psychology. The underlying desire to make the world a better place has flavored many of my life experiences. I want to do, in however small measure, what I can to improve the human condition.

Accordingly, I remain a "grassroots" Utopian, affecting the human condition one person at a time, often by listening carefully – always through love and understanding and by being honest about who I am. Occasionally, this is still difficult, yet I try not to falter. We must be truthful *especially* when it hurts, since that's when it matters most.

So it turns out that now that I'm finally back on top of my game, my country is the sickest it's ever been. When I was a kid, I'd scrape my knee and think there was nothing worse in the whole world that could happen to a person. I'd wait and wait for the scrape to heal, thinking that then my problems would finally be over once and for all. Then my grandfather died and I thought the pain would never end. At least, I reasoned, I would never have to endure anything so painful ever again. Then I was court-martialed and finally realized I had never really felt pain before. Still, I was comforted by finally knowing the worst was behind me. Then I got AIDS and discovered that the worst pain you can feel is the pain you cause others to feel.

Going through this process has made me reevaluate things a bit. Maybe life isn't so much something you have to get through – the picture is not, as we had assumed, formed by connecting the tragic dots any more than it is formed by connecting the victorious ones. Nor do we finally work our way through the end-all-be-all tragedy that signals our troubles are over and the beginning of the stress-free part our lives. After all, even the victories require work… and, yes, pain. Maybe life is rather a mix of all the above. Maybe I should stop expecting the tragedies to be over forever. Maybe the tragedies are just as important as the victories, or even part of them.

I may have started out as a random bit of an extremely outside chance, but I'm a lot more than that now. I have the wondrous and most excellent and rare ability to *affect*. I can say and do things that change other things. I can *cause*. I can make things happen. I can create…. Wow. Kind of like the way energy can come together to make matter, I can actually think up stuff that's brand spanking new.

And if I use that remarkable ability to help people live and love and be joyous, so much the better.

Hey, life is hard. And it's always going to be hard. Life is so hard, it can rip you to pieces. It can kill you, or worse, it can make you wish it had killed you. Nothing I can do or say or wish can ever change the fact that life is so gut-wrenchingly impossible that probably no one will ever completely figure it out. No one will ever be able to explain to me why people are so mean to each other. It makes my soul weep in sobs so big I can't breathe.

But I'm still breathing. I'm still fighting the good fight and I hope you'll join me. The world needs a lot of love right now. It's dark and scary out there and every one of us needs all the help we can get. Here are a few tips to get you started.

If you have AIDS, HIV, STDs, or any other life-altering or incurable illness, try to get over it (spoken gently, with a wry smile). If you're as lucky as I've been, this will take a few months, but is almost inevitable, given the quality of treatments available now.

If you're gay, lesbian, bisexual or transgender, come out. You can't truly be effective until you're honest about who you are. Don't even try to fix the world until you've fixed yourself, and being out is a vital part of that.

Then, when you're ready, go out and fix the world. Be active. Be political. Pick an issue you can be passionate about, and approach it with love and compassion. You may find yourself at risk. You may be attacked. But remember that it is a far more dangerous proposition to do nothing.

Whatever you do, never despair. Life is too rare and glorious and short... life is way too excruciatingly short... to spend it unhappily.

So do what makes you happy. For me, making other people happy does the trick nicely, but we're all (thankfully) different.

Let's spend the remainder of our lives celebrating the fact that we're all different.

Afterword

"Only in growth, reform, and change, paradoxically enough, is true security to be found."

Anne Morrow Lindbergh

I'M GRATEFUL TO HAVE BEEN ABLE TO SHARE this journey with you. Together, we've travelled through the ravages of illness to a transformation: from being an observer of the world to being an active participant. Like me, this story has evolved. Where it started as a dying man's fond farewell, it became the story about becoming a political activist and an advocate for human rights.

My arrival here was neither accidental nor a necessary result of any one experience. Many people who survive the initial onslaught of AIDS don't necessarily become activists. Like everyone else, I am a cumulative result of many influences: in my case, an austere religious upbringing, years of self-imposed guilt, an adventurous military career, a soul-smashing court-martial, and a life-long pursuit of a sense of *self*.

Now, in 2008, some may think of me as a gay-community leader. I have a pro-gay website (www.tridd.com) and a seat on the board of directors for our local health clinics. I've lobbied Congress in both our state capital and in Washington, and I've become somewhat of a gay issues "go-to guy" for the local press – and all this since I started to write the book you're now holding in your hands!

More than anything, I'm glad to report that our East Texas gay community may be starting to come out of its closet. Our secret power, which has always been in our hidden and isolated numbers, is not so hidden or isolated anymore. Our *Parents and Friends of Lesbians and Gays* (PFLAG) meetings, when I started attending, hosted no more than a half-dozen people. Now, a little more than a year later, the East Texas PFLAG chapter is still the only gay organization of any kind in all of East Texas; but our numbers are steadily growing. Just last week, we numbered forty – the biggest gathering in this group's ten-year history. It may sound silly, but I'm reminded of the time I won that stuffed dolphin at the carnival for Daniel -- that anything is possible. It makes me feel proud to think I may have had even a small role in helping my community win the prize of visibility for itself. There is a new sense around these parts that every day, things are just a little better for gays than they were the day before.

A few thoughts on freedom and security

My story has progressed, much like my life has developed, to a place where it's no longer about me, not really. My attention is now turned outside myself, to bigger issues, such as freedom for all of us.

Over the past few decades – up until September 11, 2001 – Americans enjoyed a remarkable technological and economic revolution. The personal computer has forever changed the world, connecting people in ways incomprehensible in the pre-PC era. We had also enjoyed a long period of relative peace.

More than that, we began to feel it was our birthright to feel safe. We began to equate freedom and democracy with the fact that we felt safe – and that was a big mistake.

Freedom is not safe. I would go as far as to say that freedom is diametrically opposed to safety. In terms of our children, would we prefer our three-year-old to be free or safe? I submit that we would constantly watch the three year old, forcibly protecting the child from his or her own choices and denying the child, in the process, any semblance of privacy or freedom.

But we adults prefer freedom over safety. Americans in particular have always jealously guarded our freedoms, even when it leaves gaps in our security. Police have to read suspected criminals their rights before questioning them. In America, the suspect is allowed to remain silent, even if this means we risk letting guilty people go free. Historically, Americans would rather let the guilty go free than imprison the innocent.

Freedom is dangerous. We delude ourselves if we think otherwise. But we have deluded ourselves. Unwisely thinking we could have freedom and safety, we have already begun the process of dismantling our freedom in favor of security.

We now live in a country where our phones can be wiretapped, our financial records and electronic communications viewed, and we ourselves can be indefinitely confined without cause or recourse. Our friends have begun to call us traitors for questioning all of this, even though they're the ones supporting the dismantling of the very heart of our democratic values.

Our founding fathers knew that freedom is hard won but easily lost. How did we become so cavalier with surrendering the freedoms our forefathers fought so bravely to preserve? Our birthright, as Americans, is freedom, not safety.

I, for one, prefer freedom, and I will not hold my government accountable if the cost of that freedom means that I will remain at risk. I prefer a just government over one that reduces my risk of bodily harm to zero. As inane as this must surely sound, until recent times the phrase "freedom isn't free" has never been employed to imply that the cost *is* our freedom. The cost of freedom has always been, and will remain to be, our safety, or at least our absolute safety.

When I was in high school, I remember learning about our government's use of "plausible deniability." A nervous chuckle descended over the classroom as the students realized that one of the privileges of power in America is the authority to lie. We are naïve to forget that our children learn by example – that those of us learning about our government were also learning strong lessons about morality and ethics.

When we lament the death of "family values," I suggest we look further for its killer than a loving gay community struggling for fundamental human rights. Instead, perhaps we should look at the fact that we've been teaching our children for decades that it is OK to lie, cheat and steal, since that's the way our government acts.

I may be accused of being a pacifist, even unpatriotic, but this is not the case. It is instead a profound love of my country that stirs me into motion. My purpose is to defend or in this case *recapture* our freedom. I insist, however, that the cost of that freedom cannot *be* our freedom. I insist that, while I will not hold my government accountable for my safety, I *will* hold it accountable for being truthful. They must be truthful *especially* when that truth is damaging or hurtful, so that our children may, by example, know the importance of integrity.

To paraphrase Patrick Henry, "You can have your safety. Give me liberty!" I will be neither safe nor fearful. I will not be imprisoned by my own small-mindedness. I will defend my country, but not at the cost of my integrity. I will love God, but not at the cost of reason. I understand that integrity requires courage, that there is no courage without risk. I will defend the liberties of *all* people, including the sick and disabled, and including the gay community. I am happy to be at risk when the cause is liberty – as causes go, there are none nobler.

2007 - a short story

WHERE DO I BEGIN – by saying that I am the worst criminal ever – that I have caused more deaths and pain and suffering than any other man or even war in history? You would laugh and call me a lunatic, but I know what I have done, and the world will never be the same.

You have never heard of me. I'm the anonymous guy who may have sat behind you in school, but you can't quite remember his name – an oblique silhouette from the corner of your eye that gave no cause for a second glance. Yet your life has been irreparably damaged by me. You are, in fact, far worse off as a direct result of my existence; and for that, I apologize.

If it were widely known what I have done, I would surely be put to death in the most lauded execution in the history of the world. But how could the world ever know… no one would ever believe me.

This letter is my final confession – a confession that I'm sure will go largely unheeded. I write it only to explain my suicide, and in the hope that someone, somewhere, might come to believe in what is possible… what was possible in another world – the world I came from – the world I destroyed….

I miss Douglas. He was my childhood sweetheart. To you, ours would seem an odd marriage – a marriage between science and religion – but our marriage was my reason for living. Without it… without him, I cannot bring myself to smile again.

Douglas Sanchez is… *was* a Catholic Archbishop in the Archdiocese of Chicago. We had such a life together with two beautiful, smart daughters and more than our share of contentment. I worked at the Baltain Subatomic Propulsion Development Lab, also in Chicago, on the project that killed him and countless millions of other innocents, and forever changed the face of the planet.

You will, of course, be less interested in my loss than in your own, so I will try outline a brief history of what, one short week ago, was the world in which you… all of you lived.

One week ago, the President of the United States was a black woman, Anita Thornbury. A quick internet search produces a presidential history that is largely unknown to me, so I can tell you that the presidential succession over the past hundred years, with the exceptions of Woodrow Wilson and Bill Clinton, is vastly different. Even Clinton's history is different, however. I knew nothing about a sex scandal, for example. Lost to history is the great congressional corruption cleansing of 1957, and I am unfamiliar with all the wars since the Great War, which you call WWI. There was no WWII, Korea, Vietnam, no Gulf War and no Iraq.

Just one week ago, in March of 2007, the World Trade Center stood as a shining symbol of the free market. One week ago, I had never heard of Middle Eastern terrorists or Walmart. One week ago, I drove a hydrogen-powered car and most Americans lived in smart homes and condos. Even your architecture is bleak compared to the Chicago skyline I left behind, though I have only myself to blame for the current lack of vision.

The world I left behind was largely bereft of the prejudice and disease that now seem to govern your fear and hatred. I cannot understand how hatred dominates the global attitudes and mores. If you must hate, then hate me – before I intervened last week, you were less hateful anyway.

A week ago, AIDS never happened – the terrible disease that in your history killed my husband shortly after he graduated high school in 1982. Our life together never even happened. I guess it's only fitting that the joke's on me – I am left alone, an apparent anomaly. In your world, I was never born.

In 1961, a gay man by the name of Axel Steinbrenner won the Nobel Peace Prize for his groundbreaking work on human rights, forever changing the prejudicial attitudes of much of the world's population. His "Nation of Nations" speech in 1949 was a landmark in the history of human development, leading to the most comprehensive international cooperative effort on record, virtually ending world hunger. One short week ago, his famous quote, "We are one people of many peoples" graced the marble cornerstones of many of the world's governmental buildings. Similarly, a Jewish doctor by the name of Jergen Strauss earned the world's homage in 1970 when he discovered the process by which disease mutates, leading, by 1978, to the eradication of most incurable diseases including all forms of cancer and even herpes. Of course, you have never heard of either of these men. Both of them died in concentration camps during WWII.

I mentioned earlier that there have been no major wars since the First World War, but you may never comprehend the full reality of that statement. Without expending such huge investments in war, the nations of the world grew wealthy. Poverty had been all-but eradicated. Thanks to the Global Health Initiative and Shared Health Resources Act, all of humanity enjoyed the guarantee of health care.

I'm not sure where in your history America became a global "superpower," though it seems to be largely a result of your military buildup during the Second World War. In my world, Americans were gentler in spirit. We gained some prestige through our remarkable ingenuity in the global marketplace, but did not make a habit out of throwing our weight around... militarily or otherwise. Our military strength was bolstered mainly by warm and cooperative relationships with our allies around the world.

The American congressional corruption scandal of 1957 was a turning point in American politics that brought our democracy to its knees. Some 120 members of congress were indicted for making policies based on campaign contributions and gifts from lobbyists. Of those, 92 were convicted and 58 served time in prison. As terrible a blow as it was to our national pride, what emerged was a nation much stronger. Never again would Americans place such blind faith in our elected officials. It was a wakeup call that made Americans realize the danger of unchecked power in Washington. We began by instituting procedures that encouraged transparency in the political process, valuing truth and disclosure over efficiency. This process was greatly enhanced when, in 1968, the first personal computers were made available. By 1975, 60% of the American public had access to near real-time monitors and opinion surveys of congressional activity in key areas such as education, trade issues, health, security/civil liberties, and a new website called "the Corporate Watchdog" that guarded against monopolistic practices by the largest businesses.

One week ago, Israel didn't exist, though the moderate Islamic people had allowed the reconstruction of King Solomon's Temple, making Jerusalem a huge tourist draw. Still, the nation of Palestine had a vast Jewish population and even a Jewish Secretary of State, among other key positions in that government. Moreover, Christians, Jews and Islamic people had come to believe they worship the same god, bringing all three religions into close alignment. American televangelists, like those around the world, preached about love and peace, embracing differences in all people.

Communism gradually fizzled out in the 20th century, replaced in each case by budding democratic republics. The last country to make the transition was China, in 1972. While there were many theories, it was widely believed their decision was encouraged as a prerequisite to their inclusion in the Global Health Initiative.

A colossal amount of global resources had been employed to develop extraterrestrial technologies, and already we had a colony of 120 living in a facility in lunar orbit. Several private vehicles mined rare minerals from asteroid dust, and a dedicated satellite orbited the sun inside Mercury's orbit, gathering valuable information on solar processes – a direct precursor to the technology I shall discuss in a moment.

Einstein's theories were never used to build a bomb. Instead, they were employed in a multinational initiative to develop faster-than-light transportation, which is where my story intersects the vector of human history.

Founded in 1940, the Baltain Corporation started by making hearing aids. Then, in the 1950s, they opened an advanced research facility to study sound waves. As computer technology advanced throughout the 1960s, they branched out into sound and light wave research, which put them in a position of opportunity when, in 1984, the "Faster than Light" global transportation initiative was formed and funded. Baltain, having the best light wave research facilities in the world, was easily chosen by the multinational committee to win the contract for propulsion development.

The idea was, obviously, fast transportation. The benefits of such technology were profound and infinite... from delivering product and supplies to medevac to mass evacuations during natural disasters to vacations to business to interstellar exploration and travel. The list of benefits was endless – the downside was zero. Or so we thought.

I came to work for Baltain in 1995 as a project manager after a highly competitive interview process. Ironically, I wouldn't have even been looking for jobs in Chicago had Douglas not been recently assigned there by the Catholic Church as a priest. But there I was, applying for one of the most sought-after positions in the world – on the cutting edge of the faster-than-light initiative. I never really asked why I was selected from the hundreds of applicants. I suppose the fact I had been a Rhodes Scholar didn't hurt; or my subatomic light particle research experience, or the fact I had served on the National Technology Advisory Council. My guess is that I was comfortable enough, in the fourth round of interviews, to tell a self-effacing joke about two scientists and a golfer.

I was in charge of four propulsion groups, and over the years we made tremendous progress bending spatial fields. The eyes of the world were upon us as we conquered issue after issue, gradually progressing toward what was widely believed to be imminent success.

Our counterparts in other fields progressed as well. Vehicle design, assigned to Protidyne, a French company, was in the final stages by 2006, as was the energy contractor. Energy had, interestingly, become a major focal point in the overall scheme of the project, given the enormous amount required to make any of this work. The generator, developed by Eaton Energy Corp in Seattle, utilized a fascinating technology called "symbolic fusion" to amplify fusion reactions to millions of times more powerful than that produced in typical fusion reactors. Still, the problem of stored energy was a major one. In order to be effective, the device would have to be able to store enough energy for a single return trip. Most faster-than-light journeys would need to return to their point of origin, and one of our basic parameters was to presume that the destination points would not necessarily have symbolic fusion power available. We briefly looked at placing a reactor on the vehicle itself, but this was not possible due to size and a frightening potential for disaster known as the "Eaton paradox." Simply put, the paradox is similar to trying to lift yourself off the ground by pulling on your own hair.

So before we could make our first "test flight" we had to solve the problem of energy storage… enough energy to return to the point of origin. Here, the project bogged down for months, until Mathias Billings, a seventeen-year-old prodigy at MIT, hit upon an idea. Our paradigm had always focused on capacitors and traditional battery storage, which was a mistake. Mathias solved the problem by starting at the finishing point – having scooped up energy along the initial voyage, like a wind-up toy. The process easily stored more energy than we would need, since the physics of field bending provided for a return trip that was vastly more energy-friendly than the initial field disruption. We were therefore able to place a modified fusion reactor aboard the vessel. The reactor was to "store" the energy of the initial journey as a kind of subatomic "memory," which would then be "played back" for the return flight.

All of this was so revolutionary that no one considered the necessary repercussions of the design. It wasn't until February of 2007, as I sat staring blankly at a particular algorithm on my computer screen, that it hit me. The "storage reactor" wasn't simply storing field-bending energy… it was storing *time*! I grew instantly dizzy with the ramifications of my revelation – oblivious even to a drop of drool I had allowed to escape from my mouth. I reached up to wipe my lip at the precise moment the droplet landed on a sheet of paper as it materialized from nowhere.

Yeah… I said "from nowhere." On my desk was a sheet of paper that had not been there a moment before, upon which settled a small, moist droplet of drool, and on which had been scrawled, in my handwriting, the words "Destroy this document immediately, then make another one just like it and send it back."

I sat staring at the document, perfectly motionless, feeling as if I could not move. How treacherous was the landscape over which I now gazed – how infinite the potential for disaster? How could I, in my right mind, allow our grand experiment to continue? Would not any thinking, ethical person immediately sabotage the project? Would not even my own life be a miniscule price to pay to prevent this

technology from being exploited to the detriment of humanity...
indeed, of all life?

But then I realized that my decision had already been made. I
had already decided to continue; else the paper would not have
appeared on my desk. I realized at length that my scientific curiosity
was more powerful than my fear -- I had elected to peer briefly
through the looking glass – to see what no one had seen before. I
would move through time. But I would proceed with caution. I
would start with something small, a piece of paper, for example.

It was growing late. Most of my comrades had left for the day.
How could I completely destroy the page in front of me, I wondered,
leaving no trace... no potential for paradoxes unknown – the
possible paradox of simultaneous existence of identical matter, for
example? Just to be safe, I didn't want any molecular trace of the
page on my desk to exist at the same moment in time as the page I
was about to write. At length, I chose the reactor. With tweezers, I
carefully placed the page into the expansion chamber of the symbolic
fusion reactor we had on the premises, knowing all molecular traces
of the paper would be consumed in the process of going on line. (In
retrospect, my excessive caution was likely unnecessary, since the
sheet of paper is itself a different object from one instant in time to
the next, given the fact of its constant molecular motion.)

Then I pulled, from a fresh ream, a sheet on which I scribbled
the words: "Destroy this document immediately, then make another
one just like it and send it back."

First, I considered that the proximity of all the destinations involved in my initial experiment would allow for the page to be sent remotely, without the need to be accompanied by the transportation vessel. I set the equipment for faster than light travel to our test facility on the other side of the Baltain Development facility, then proceeded to the "memory reactor" that powered and controlled the return trip. Here, I imposed the algorithm that would make the return anything but typical – setting coordinates slightly above the surface of my desk and forcing the presumed constant, which literally described the speed of time, to be instead a variable quantity. I couldn't help but smile at how elegant the algorithm appeared on the screen – like a page of music in Mozart's own handwriting. And like Mozart, the only thing better than the manuscript's proposition of music is the playing of it – the effect of the music transcending its beauty on the printed page.

It was a truly bizarre, if somewhat anticlimactic, sensation… dutifully transmitting the page I had already received and destroyed, the only proof of my success having been witnessed hours earlier. I stared blankly at the empty transmission chamber, considering my next move.

"Caution," I thought. Moving through time was fraught with danger beyond reason. Fearful of the repercussions of the technology in the wrong hands, I resolved to keep my secret to myself… at least for the time being. Furthermore, I knew that any experiment would require the utmost caution against altering the past in any appreciable way. Any incursions into the past, I knew, must be observational only. Great care would need to be taken not to materially vary prior events.

So I asked myself, with some glee, what event in history I would most like to observe. My first thoughts were of Abraham Lincoln. By way of researching my subject, I looked him up and printed out a few paragraphs from the history. Little did I know that these few paragraphs would soon hold the only dubious "proof" that my world – *the* world – had ever existed.

"Against strong opposition, Abraham Lincoln (1809-1901), at the conclusion of the Civil War in 1865, insisted on a gentle, loving approach to southern "reparations," resisting the northern consensus that a more severe response was called for. His tempered approach, including the recognition of many existing Southern state governments, led to a quick re-integration of the South into the Union. His policy of the "Fruits of Forgiveness" ultimately made him the only candidate acceptable by both North and South during the Presidential campaign of 1868, leading to his unprecedented election to a third term. To this day, Lincoln is remembered as the only American President to serve more than two terms in office.

"Most importantly, Lincoln is remembered as the President whose gentle approach to postwar reparations led to a more stable postwar environment, reducing hostilities still felt by the South. This approach and the post Civil War successes felt here in America would have a profound effect on twentieth century politics around the world, most notably the Treaty of Versailles after the Great War.

"Lincoln had been friends with Walt Whitman (1819-1892) since 1869, when Whitman was still working in Washington. In 1873, Whitman suffered a stroke and moved to Camden, New Jersey to convalesce. Lincoln followed suit by moving to Philadelphia, just across the Delaware River from Camden, in 1880 following the death of his wife, Mary Todd Lincoln. Their friendship flourished after that, with frequent afternoon meetings at various Camden restaurants.

"In 1887, the Saturday Evening Post ran a story about Lincoln and Whitman that referred to the two gentlemen collectively as "Those Grand Old Men"—a moniker that came to define a new category of acquaintanceship between two men. Though their sexuality was not spoken of, Whitman's and Lincoln's friendship in their later years was embraced even during their lives as an archetype of a relationship between two uniquely American minds. Their subsequent essays, both individually and co-authored, skirting the issues of same-sex friendship and even sensuality, struck a nerve in an emerging American gentility; and they had unwittingly begun the process of mitigating prejudice against homosexuals. In later years, they will be viewed by most as founders of the gay civil liberties movement. Lincoln in particular gained iconic status as a cultural hero among proponents of gay rights.

"Interestingly, neither man ever publicly admitted homosexual tendencies. Whitman rejected the thought outright, while Lincoln took the high road and refused to respond to such questions altogether. Both men are forgiven for their position on the subject, however, given the puritanical atmosphere of the era. Such topics were not considered proper in "polite society."

"In 1882, a young Oscar Wilde (1854-1920) paid a visit to Whitman, whose "Leaves of Grass" had already gained enormous popularity around the world and was especially inspirational to the gay culture in Britain in the late 19th century. There, he met Lincoln, with whom he kept correspondence until Lincoln's death in 1901.

"In 1905, Wilde produced a comedy entitled "Those Grand old Men," ostensibly about the relationship between Lincoln and Whitman. The play was poorly received, however, and closed after only a week in London, yet it left a lasting impression and later became a cult classic within the emerging gay culture. While it made no explicit reference to sex, its comedic inferences were unmistakable and considered in poor taste by conservative audiences of the time."

Over the following few days, I said nothing to anyone of my revelatory experiment, but set about the task of secretly planning my next move – a short excursion into history. My original hope of observing that famous meeting between Lincoln, Whitman and Wilde was too fraught with danger – the danger my presence might cause a disruption of their private histories. A public appearance, I considered, would provide the best opportunity for an observation unnoticed and unaffecting the course of events that must follow. Ultimately, I settled on Lincoln's speech at the conclusion of the Civil War... the one where he began to lay out his vision of reconstructing the Union, just days before the thwarted assassination attempt by John Wilkes Booth.

On the morning of Tuesday, March 13, 2007, I kissed Douglas goodbye and packed our daughters in the car for the ride to school. After the kiss, my gaze lingered on him for a moment and he asked me, "Is everything all right?"

"Yes," I responded. "I just have a lot on my mind. Have I told you today how much I love you?"

"As a matter of fact, you have," he smiled, "but only twice."

"Third time's a charm," I said, as I walked out the door.

That vision of him, standing there in the doorway, is stamped in my memory like an indictment. It was the last time I would ever see him.

I was late getting to work that day, having stopped to purchase from a theatrical costuming company some period clothing and from a numismatic firm about a hundred dollars in period currency and coin. How stupid I was not to have brought a tiny video recorder… but I had much on my mind and was mainly concerned with not altering history.

Our faster-than-light transportation project was, for all practical purposes, finished. We had sent live animals from one side of the vast Baltain complex to the other and back again without a hitch. Press releases had been digested by the world's population, though as with any major technological innovation, few had truly considered the benefits they would soon enjoy from it. Soon, transportation would be as easy and as inexpensive as a phone call or an email.

Still, the corporate rollout process can be cumbersome. The first human transmission would be televised and coordinated with political leaders and movie stars and, of course, scientists. I had myself become quite a celebrity over the previous few months, especially since the project assembly from the various contractors had been assigned to our Chicago facility. All of this had placed me in the best position, among all those great minds who put the project together, for interviews and (dare I say) public adoration.

The members of my four teams found all of this public attention quite humorous, and took the opportunity to chide me at every turn. "Hey, hero," was a common greeting at work, and this particular morning, I found a note taped to my monitor. It was a checklist of things to do, all of which had been checked off as complete. The list started with "drop kids off at school," and "pick up laundry," and ended with "change the world."

We were all preoccupied that day with preparations for the project's televised global rollout in two weeks. My personal preoccupation therefore went largely unnoticed – the preoccupation with my secret journey, this evening, through time.

As was my habit, I hung around the office after work, waiting for the building to clear out. At 6:30, I retrieved the 1860 clothes from my briefcase and prepared for the trip.

The vessel, dubbed the *Proteus* by its designing firm, Protidyne, looks a bit like an elongated pewter-colored egg on its side... considered a fitting model, since the project represented the birth of a new era in transportation. Our prototype... the one you'll find in an overgrown field just west of your current Chicago, was large enough for only a single person, though future models were blueprinted to carry hundreds.

My first task was to get enough stored-up energy in the memory reactor to both convert to time and to return home. Accordingly, I set the unmanned vessel for transmission to a point in space about halfway to Neptune's orbit and back. The vessel was gone only a few seconds, and I was almost surprised when it returned undamaged with enough surplus energy to penetrate a hundred twenty years of history, just as I had planned.

I chose a location just north of Washington, in what, according to some Civil War sketches, was a thicket of trees. I set up the failsafe for "unsurveyed destination" to prevent myself from materializing inside a tree or a hill – since even a blade of grass could cause dire and unpredictable results – then the date of April 11, 1865 and a time of 4:00 am. In the unlikely event that I could not return, I also set the memory reactor to return automatically on the morning of April 12, with or without me, so that no trace of the equipment would be left behind.

Wearing the black pants, waistcoat and white shirt I had purchased at the theatrical shop, I emptied my pockets of all but the antique cash and a copy of a Civil War era map. For some reason, I also elected to carry the few pages of history I had printed out. In retrospect, it was a stupid thing to do, though now I'm happy to have them, since they are all I have left of my world.

I barely hesitated, once I found myself sitting in the prototype, to initiate the startup sequence. Once the reactors were online, I received the three green lights that signaled system readiness. The label on the fateful button was comically straightforward... like an old-fashioned fax machine; it simply read, "Send."

Nothing happened at first, besides an odd deja-vu sort of subjective experience that time was slowing. It felt very much like those last instants of time before one is involved in a car accident, when every detail seems to slow as the adrenaline rushes through your mind, watching the offending vehicle plow toward you. The first thing I noticed was the sensation in my ears that the ambient sounds in the room were fading, or rather "stopped up," as when your head dips beneath the surface of a pool. This was followed by a ripple in my field of view that, starting at the front of the craft, quickly enveloped everything. For a moment, I felt weightless, then immediately my weight returned to me, exactly as though my car had just crested a small hill....

It was dark outside, the lights of the test facility conspicuously absent... the only illumination provided by my instrument panel. I heard the sound of what must have been the branch of a tree scraping gently against the side of the craft and, beneath that, the slow drip of water on leaves. It was raining.

My excursion, I realized, had been poorly planned. It was dark and it was raining and I had no flashlight, no umbrella, no compass.... I hadn't even packed a lunch. But I didn't care. I was lost in a late nineteenth century forest six miles north of the White House, and all I could think was, "I'm actually here!"

Given my circumstances, it would have been pointless to leave the dry safety of the vessel, so I resolved to wait for first light. The clock on the instrument panel read "2013," or 8:13 pm – the time when I departed from Chicago – but I knew it was 4:00 am now, and I knew that sunrise in Washington, DC on April 11, 1865 was at 5:32 am, giving me an hour and a half to calm down and collect my thoughts. I powered down the vessel, and sat in the darkness; the drip-drip-dripping of the rain marking time, like a grandfather clock in the foyer of some great Victorian house.

Gradually, the dripping slowed, and then stopped altogether. Gradually, my eyes adjusted to the darkness, and the outlines of trees emerged, silhouetted against the emerging glow of the early morning sky. I slid back the door just as the sound of a distant rooster announced the arrival of morning in the otherwise silent environs.

Since I had placed myself just west of a north/south running road on my map, I headed out in the general direction of the rising sun – my footsteps through the forest bramble muted by moisture. The cool air smelled sweet and clean. The more distance I put between myself and the *Proteus*, the more I felt at home, considering myself, for the time-being, a resident-in-fact of Lincoln's milieu.

Finally, after about a half-mile of trudging through the thick, hilly underbrush, I came upon a clearing that bordered a finely constructed dirt road; built up to better shed rainwater. There, I headed south, picking up my pace a bit, and quickly came upon an intersection with a smaller road that led off to my right. A short, hand painted wooden sign read "J Seldon."

Within a quarter mile, I came upon what appeared to be a roadside stand or farmer's market, a small wooden roofed structure with no walls and enclosed only by tables on three sides. As I drew closer, a sign on one of the posts revealed it to be a toll booth, though it was currently unmanned. The booth sat at an intersection, providing options of one left turn toward the northeast, two right turns headed northwest and southwest, or continuing on my present path, which headed almost due south. The roads were labeled "Milkhouse Ford," and "Blagden's Mill," and revealed that my current path was called "Georgia Ave." Beyond the intersection, more private drives and a few farm houses close to the road indicated a more densely populated area. I was getting close to town.

After walking another mile down Georgia Avenue, I was startled to hear the sound of singing. Within a few minutes, I was just able to make out the words: "The Union forever," the song went, "hurrah, boys, hurrah. Down with the traitor, up with the star as we rally 'round the flag, boys, rally once again, shouting the battle cry of freedom." And now I could see a small detachment of twenty or so soldiers, wearing Union blues and carrying packs and rifles as they walked across the road from my left to right. By the time I arrived at the intersection at which they had crossed, they were a few hundred feet down a road called "Rock Cr." The sign in that direction read "U.S. Military Asylum," and the one on my path read "Washington 2 Mi." Hearing horse's hooves, I turned to see a horse-drawn wagon, laden with produce, headed toward town. "Good morning," I shouted as the driver passed me. "Good morning to you, sir," the driver responded, tipping his straw hat. By now, a few dogs were barking as well. Washington was waking up.

By the time I reached Florida Avenue, another mile or so down the road, I had been joined in my journey toward town by some twenty fellow pedestrians of various ages, some traveling alone, and others in groups of two and three. Every few minutes, another horsedrawn cart would pass, as well as the faster horseback riders, both civilian and military. Florida Avenue represented a clear demarcation between city and country, the land to the north clearly divided into farms, while the area to the south was composed of smaller lots, containing rows of white one- and two-story homes. Here, the street signs were professionally made. It began to dawn on me that I actually had traveled back in time. I took a deep breath of the sweet air. Exhaling, I said "Welcome to Washington," out loud.

The air was filled with the smells of breakfast, awakening in me a powerful hunger, and I rapidly revised my plans to include a meal. While I had originally planned no contact whatsoever, my earlier greeting got me thinking that some minor contact would be unlikely to alter the course of history. A passing greeting or one additional customer in a restaurant would not, I considered at length, cause any great tragic changes in the path of human events to follow. Now, through the window of hindsight, my naiveté looks criminal.

Just inside Washington proper, Georgia Ave. became 7th Street, and precisely at the intersection of 7th and G Streets, the dirt pavement gave way to cobblestone, and the homes to businesses. I was downtown. By now, the streets were alive with activity, people of all sorts hurriedly walked or rode hurriedly to and fro. On the outskirts, the flow of traffic had been *toward* town, though here, it would be hard to discern the most popular direction. The business signs were straightforward, composed of a single word, such as "Meats." Some added a family brand, such as "C Miller, Dry Goods."

The noise level was now significantly higher as well, hooves clacking on cobblestone, and voices echoing off brick buildings. The air downtown was decidedly rank, which surprised me. It smelled of horse feces and spoiling produce and meat and even a twinge of human urine. The odor was offensive at first, but after a few minutes I didn't notice it.

From the corner of 7th Street and Pennsylvania Avenue, my view revealed the Capitol Building to my left; to my right, in the distance, an oblique view of the White House. All along Pennsylvania avenue, street vendors were setting up carts and improvised stands to sell all varieties of goods, from foodstuffs to housewares to presidential and Civil War souvenirs, such as postcards and figurines. A block further to the south I crossed a bridge over a man-made canal to a vast grassy mall and a view of the Washington Monument, which was unfinished. Just south of the mall, a train whistled as it slowly eased southward.

I headed back toward Pennsylvania Avenue, where I found a small restaurant, abuzz with conversation and frenetic with activity. Sitting on a stool at the counter, I found it easy to determine the most popular topics of conversation. The Civil War had just been won, and everyone was talking about it. "General Grant," and "Abe

Lincoln" frequently rose above the din of conversation. Someone said, "…calls himself a Republican," to which a response was yelled, "Whatever happened to the Whigs," resulting in a short burst of laughter. The atmosphere was jubilant… relieved… though I noticed a few silent, lone patrons who seemed more perturbed than celebratory – dark faces turned downward toward the task of eating. The accents were decidedly less "American" than I had expected, sounding more like their parent British, German, Irish or Italian dialects.

I ordered pancakes, eggs and sausage, along with a cup of coffee, absorbing the experience as easily as I devoured the food. The tab came to thirty-five cents, which I paid with a worn half-dollar coin. My change; a dime, a two-cent and a three-cent coin, dated 1864, 1861 and 1862 respectively, were as shiny and new as if they had just been pressed the day before.

I spent the remainder of the morning on a walking tour of the city, stopping for a few minutes to get my shoes shined and to clear the mud from my feet. After dusting my trouser legs, the shoeshine man, who spoke with a thick Irish brogue, remarked, "Those are a fine pair of shoes, sir. Might I inquire where you purchased them?"

"In Boston," I lied, "though I can't recall the maker."

"Well, I've never seen a finer pair," he added, increduously.

To this, I added my thanks and hurried off. My shoes, a pair of black casuals, were in fact of modern make. I had presumed no one would notice them.

By 11:00 am I found myself sitting exhausted on a park bench on the national mall. My feet were weary and the rest was most welcome. The grounds were beautifully landscaped, with trees and ponds and undulating footpaths, all of which led, ultimately to a castle-like structure – the Smithsonian.

As I approached the building, I saw a man hanging a notice near the museum's great doors, announcing Lincoln's public appearance this very evening at the White House. Spectators were instructed to gather on the front lawn at 6:30 pm to hear "the President's pronouncement of the end of war and measures proposed to restore the Union States."

Inside, the Smithsonian was largely a museum of natural history. Chief on display were the fruits of the Wilkes Expedition, a U.S. Navy exploration of the Southern Seas between 1838 and 1842, which had amassed thousands of specimens of flora, fauna and minerals from the South Pacific. Before seeing this exhibit, I had not realized its importance in our early understanding of the Pacific Ocean, from Rio to Antarctica; from an accurate mapping of the West Coast to a comprehensive overland route that far surpassed, in detail of discovery, the famous Lewis and Clark Expedition.

The Smithsonian visit had left me famished. It was almost 2:00 pm. I stopped into Gautier's Restaurant, on Pennsylvania Avenue, since it appeared to be the most elegant option in the vicinity. The menu was impressive, if a bit pricier than my thirty-five cent breakfast. As a first course I had options ranging from game soup to carrot soup to soles a la crème. Entrees included curried rabbit, pigeon pie, larks and potato or pigs feet with truffles. More exotic items graced the second and third courses, including "tongue garnished," roast hare, and mince pies. Feeling ambitious, I ordered the game soup, rabbit, and boiled turkey and celery sauce, which was delicious, and a pint of ale to wash it down. Finally sated, I sat back and watched the busy foot traffic outside the restaurant's large, curtained windows. A few elegant ladies strolled leisurely by, but most of the pedestrians were in a hurry -- many important things to be done in this capital city on this auspicious day. I was shaken from my wonderings by a sudden clap of thunder, followed by the lower, rolling variety. I paid my check, which came to $4.25, left a handsome tip of one dollar and set out to purchase an umbrella.

A short walk brought me to the W.W.Corcoran Haberdashery, a narrow storefront on Maryland Avenue specializing in gentlemen's accoutrements. It was primarily a hat store, and there I found all varieties of headgear, from top hats to derbies to gaucho hats to bowlers. I selected a tan topper, which was shorter than a proper top hat, with a slight flare at the crown. With my intended purchase on my head, I browsed through a selection of combs made of horn and toothbrushes with wood or bone handles. For children, the store also offered a "Bilbo Catcher," a simple amusement made by attaching a wooden ball and spindle by means of a short length of string. The object was, apparently, to catch the ball on the cupped end of the spindle. Finally, I selected a fine, silver-handled umbrella, completed my purchase and stepped outside just as the first drops of rain began to fall.

Somewhere in the distance, a clock tower chimed five o'clock. My appointment with President Lincoln was drawing near. The poor planning of my excursion once again crossed my mind as the stores around town closed and I realized I had failed to purchase a kerosene lamp to help me find my way back to the *Proteus*.

I wandered through the streets and parks near the White House for the following hour as city employees went about raising the gas flames in numerous street lamps and an audience began to gather on the White House lawn. By six o'clock, the rain had subsided to a barely detectable drizzle, replacing in the process most of the complex smells of the city with the familiar scent of moist earth. The damp air also cocooned in a softer version the sharp sound of hooves and wagon wheels on cobblestone.

The audience was in a chatty mood this evening, and there was much to discuss. I took up a position at the rear of the gathering crowd, behind two young women wearing evening hooped dresses. I soon found myself next to a handsome young goateed man who was quite well dressed. "Good evening," I offered, almost yelling to be heard over the mounting clamor.

"Good evening to you," he replied, unsmiling.

Off to my left, a middle-aged man was engaged in a debate with a small group of acquaintances. "The South must be made to repair what they have broken," he yelled. This remark, heard over a momentary lull in the overall commotion, resulted in a brief celebratory applause across the throng. Other discussions mentioned

Jefferson Davis, the Battle of Five Forks, and the inevitable complaints that the President was running later than the advertised appearance time of six thirty.

Trying to make small talk, I asked my young friend, "What is your opinion of the current state of affairs?"

"I am, my good man, for what is just and right," was his curt response.

By a quarter of seven, the lawn was full, with more people gathering in and across the street, even spilling over onto the national mall. My position was now toward the front and in the center, providing a better view of the balcony than most. From time to time, a call for Lincoln would rise and fall through various parts of the multitude – like a mindless religious chant, they would repeat, "Lincoln, Lincoln, Lincoln," rhythmically, until they seemingly grew bored and the chanting died out, only to start up again a few minutes later in another part of the mass.

The White House was abundantly lit with scores of gas lamps, which cast a dim glow over the assemblage in the encroaching misty darkness.

When the clock tower struck seven o'clock, the crowd's impatience grew, and everyone joined the chanting, which ceased abruptly only when the President suddenly appeared on the second floor balcony. Next came his twelve-year-old son, Tad, a few officials and a man who seemed, by his readied writing implements, to be a reporter.

What had moments earlier been a raucous assemblage now stood completely silent. But for the sound of a dog barking some few blocks away, we might have heard the distant ocean waves lapping against the shore.

The President was also silent, a tall, gaunt figure standing in the authority of deep contemplation, sizing up an audience that easily extended beyond the realm of his vision.

Finally, Lincoln turned toward the reporter and nodded perfunctorily, to which the reporter responded by stepping forward, holding a kerosene lantern out to better illuminate the pages of notes the President now held against the balcony's railing.

"We meet this evening," he began, "not in sorrow, but in gladness of heart. The evacuation of Petersburg and Richmond, and the surrender of the principal insurgent army, give hope of a righteous and speedy peace whose joyous expression cannot be restrained."

The audience remained utterly silent, intent on hearing every word as the great man's presentation began, though I heard a strong sigh from the young man to my right, who seemed oddly perturbed as he shifted his weight from one leg to the other.

In 1865, the world was still several decades from the inventions that would enable the recording of the human voice, and I had only guessed at what Lincoln may have sounded like, but now I listened intently, not to a re-creation by an actor, but to the man himself, with his peculiar style and inflections. The reality of it gave me goose bumps. He spoke in a way that can best be described as *considered* –

each phrase carefully planned and delivered for maximum effect. Moreover, he spoke with a kind of affection that a father might reserve for his children, conveying a profound lesson or message of integrity. Unlike many of the voices I had heard on this day, his accent was distinctly American. He talked like a country boy with country diction, but this only served to magnify his mastery of the English language.

"Unlike a case of a war between independent nations," he continued, "there is no authorized organ for us to treat with. No one man has authority to give up the rebellion for any other man."

From time to time, the completed pages would drop to the balcony floor, where they were dutifully retrieved by the young Tad Lincoln, after which Tad returned to his father's side, peering in silent astonishment over the mass of people, who were ourselves enthralled by the realization that we were witnessing a truly historic moment in time.

"It is also unsatisfactory to some that the elective franchise is not given to the colored man. I would myself prefer that it were now conferred on the very intelligent, and on those who serve our cause as soldiers."

The young man to my right grew increasingly anxious at this part of the speech, making an unintelligible remark under his breath. A burly working class gentleman next to him seemed now quite perturbed himself and said to him quietly, "Would you please be quiet!"

The President continued: "Some twelve thousand voters in the heretofore slave-state of Louisiana have sworn allegiance to the Union, assumed to be the rightful political power of the State, held elections, organized a State government, adopted a free-state constitution, giving the benefit of public schools equally to black and white, and empowering the Legislature to confer the elective franchise upon the colored man. Their Legislature has already voted to ratify the constitutional amendment recently passed by Congress, abolishing slavery throughout the nation."

The suggestion that any blacks should be allowed to vote was apparently too much for the man to my right to stomach. "No!" he shouted, loudly enough that the President himself surely heard it. "That is the last speech he will make."

The burly man next to him had also had enough of his interruptions. "You, sir, are no gentleman," he responded, as he shoved the young man into me so hard that he knocked both of us onto the damp earth. This caused some commotion as everyone in our immediate vicinity turned to see what was going on. The two young women in hoop dresses were particularly fascinated, one of them excitedly saying to the other, "Look! That's the actor, John Wilkes Booth!"

"I am most terribly sorry, my dear sir," said Mr. Booth to me as he quickly jumped to his feet and offered his hand. "Are you all right?"

My mind was spinning. I knew I had heard that name somewhere, but I'm embarrassed to admit I could not at first place him. I rose off the ground without his assistance, to which he responded, "My views are apparently unwelcome here. I bid you good evening." Brushing his hands together as if to wash the entire affair from memory, he exited by way of the back of the crowd, toward the uncompleted Washington Monument.

"John Wilkes Booth," I mumbled to myself as the President concluded his presentation. "Where do I know that name?" And then it hit me. A mere footnote in history, Mr. Booth was famous for his botched assassination attempt. If memory served, the poorly planned attempt was easily averted because of the suspicious attention he had drawn toward himself at a local theater. His sprained wrist, bandaged in white, had apparently acted like a beacon during the darkened performance, and he had been tackled by a bodyguard even as he raised the pistol toward the back of Lincoln's head.

Your history records a quite different tale. In your history, Booth's attempt was better planned. In your history, his routine had not been interrupted and he went to the theater hours before the play "Our American Cousin" to check his mail, where he learned of Lincoln's plans to attend. In your history, Booth's wrist was never sprained. In your history, his fall was softened by landing on me!

At the time, I only knew about the *potential* for disaster my presence might have set into motion, though I had no way of knowing the fact of it. Still, my face flushed, my heart pounded, my breath quickened with the realization that I had just made contact with an historical figure with possibly toxic historic consequences. If I could have guessed at even a fraction of the effect my presence was about to have, I would not have bothered returning to the present day.

But I didn't know. I knew only that I should never have come in the first place. Erroneously believing that I might, by means of a hasty exit, mitigate any damage my existence in this time might have set into motion, I hastily made my way back toward the *Proteus*.

Long past sunset, the darkened environs of Washington suddenly looked alien and hostile. Where I had once felt like a welcome resident, I now felt foul and poisonous to these unsuspecting victims of my folly.

Back on 7th Street, I saw a middle-aged man with a kerosene lantern, for which I offered the outrageous sum of fifty dollars. The incredulous gentleman instantly accepted my proposal and I, heart pounding through my chest, continued northward at a pace just short of a dead run.

"Please, God," I silently prayed over and over, "don't let my actions change history."

Within a half-hour, I came across a familiar road sign, marking the property of J Seldon. A short distance further, I recognized, even in the dimly moonlit darkness, the small clearing I first came across after leaving the *Proteus*. I knew I would probably have to wait for first light before finding the *Proteus*. Still, I left the safety of the road, hoping against hope that I would find the machine, and end up sleeping in my own bed tonight.

Using my umbrella to hold back the underbrush, I made my way through the mucky terrain, and was surprised after only twenty minutes to come across one of my own footprints, aimed in the opposite direction, neatly stamped into the forest floor and full of water. Looking straight ahead, I could just make out a shimmer of moonlight reflected off the egg-shaped prototype vessel. I allowed myself, in that brief moment, to believe that no harm had been done. Soon, I thought, I would be home, and all would be well.

In retrospect, I suppose I was fortunate to have forgotten to disengage the "unsurveyed destination" failsafe before returning to the present. Fortunate inasmuch as that the "present" I was returning to was indeed unsurveyed. Had I disengaged that particular failsafe, which allowed for variations in the destination coordinates, I would have, as it turns out, materialized inside a large oak tree. But I didn't. My craft instead "returned" to the present day in a field just adjacent to said tree, in a place just west of Chicago where, in my world, was part of the enormous Baltain Subatomic Propulsion Development Lab.

For my part, I had no idea where or even *when* I was… only that I recognized nothing… only that my craft had expended the last of its stored energy to get here… only that I had been awake and fully engaged and active for over twenty-four hours… only that I was far too tired to try to solve my current predicament. After a quick walk around the immediate area, I crawled back into the craft, choked back my tears, and immediately fell asleep.

The details of the following day are now a blur in my memory. Most of it was spent walking in my ridiculous costume down various roads and highways, trying to get back to Chicago. I remember futile searches through phonebooks for any vestige of the people and places I left behind. My little remaining currency proved useless, and I finally came across a homeless shelter, where I was served a meal and given a place to sleep. I was, of course, found by everyone I met to be quite insane.

On the second day, I pawned my hat and umbrella and sold my antique coins and remaining Civil War currency to a coin shop, the proceeds from which I used to purchase an outfit from a second-hand clothes store. Then I went to a public library, where I took up the study of currently available technologies.

The storage reactor on my prototype vessel is useless in your world. Trying to use it would be like rubbing a fluorescent tube across a carpet in King Henry's court. You may get a flicker out of it if you could get it near light speed, but without a very different form of energy than now exists on this planet – without the ability to send it perpendicularly across spatial fields – it will never again be operational. With only the most rudimentary understanding of nuclear fusion, your occasional and inefficient fission reactors seem to act as a band aide for an energy infrastructure that still relies primarily on fossil fuels. In my world, oil had long ago been abandoned as a Victorian energy source. Even if you had mastered fusion, it would have merely provided a starting point – a launching paradigm from which the notion of symbolic fusion might have been imagined. My background in propulsion rather than energy technologies serves only as a further symptom of our collective misfortune. I haven't the foggiest idea how to help you get from where you are to where we were. My machine runs on *time*, and no one present has any better understanding how to generate it than a caveman would have understood how to power an electric blender. On your current path, it may be millennia before such minds come together again to create such potentialities.

My third day in your world was also my second day in the library, though I now focused my attention on your post-Civil War history. Lincoln was, as you know, assassinated. He never met Oscar Wilde and never unwittingly facilitated an early acceptance of gay and lesbian culture. Even if I or Archbishop Sanchez had lived in your world, we would have been prohibited from marrying by both your legalized discrimination and by the Catholic Church. Nor would we have been permitted to adopt our beautiful daughters.

The differences in our histories are so numerous that I find little value, at this point, in exploring them in detail. Of major significance, however, is your use of hatred and violence to "solve" your political and cultural problems. This dysfunctional approach can be traced, I believe, to one of the major turning points when our respective global histories took irrevocably divergent paths.

At the conclusion of World War I, the leaders of four countries met in Versailles, France to discuss the post-war treatment of a defeated Germany and its people. These leaders, in both of our histories, were Prime Minister David Lloyd George of the United Kingdom, President Georges Clemenceau of France, Vittorio Orlando of Italy, and President Woodrow Wilson of the United States. Of primary importance to President Wilson in your history was the establishment of a "League of Nations," and he was willing to concede most of his remaining "fourteen points" to realize this singular aim. His concessions necessarily included a vastly kinder treatment of postwar Germany, as Clemenceau insisted was necessary.

Given his preoccupation with the League of Nations, Wilson deferred to France, and the people of Germany were made to suffer for their arrogant play for world dominance. Accordingly, huge chunks of German territory were given over to its neighboring states, the German military was restricted to the size of a modest police force and Germany was required to pay the then-enormous sum of 6.6 billion British pounds. In addition, all German ocean liners, locomotives, commercial motor vehicles, factory equipment and much else was confiscated. In other words, Germany was first made to pay for the war and then deprived of the means to generate payment. Even your historians are in agreement that the severe conditions of the Versailles Treaty created, in Germany, the resentment which made possible Hitler's subsequent rise to power and the resulting chaos and destruction you know as the second World War.

In my history, however, Wilson was far more interested in global post-war recovery than a League of Nations, and he had good reason. Using the American model successfully implemented by Lincoln after the Civil War, he convinced Britain and Italy (who had also studied the Lincolnian approach) that the "Fruits of Forgiveness" would yield a vastly more stable future for all concerned parties, and they were right.

When I compare our divergent histories, I find the Treaty of Versailles to be a critical moment when humanity chose hate over love as a policy. The religions and governments of your history since that crucial moment are defined more frequently by common enemies than by common interests.

You are alien to me. Though you continue to suffer for your decisions, you clutch your hatreds close to your hearts… you are addicted to them, holding them as dear as your children. Hatred colors your media, your technology, your politics and your economics, and it is utterly my fault.

The world in which you live was never supposed to be. It is an error… an aberration… an abomination of what should have been… what was and what can never be again. I only hope that you will at least strive to get back to even the slightest approximation of the potential I have erased.

Index

abolition of slavery · 175
abomination · 121, 122, 205
abort · 190, 191
abort the takeoff · 190
absorbing information · 205
abstinence only · 121
absurd · 36, 46, 69, 127
absurdity · 105
abysmal progress · 116
Academic Freedom · 107
academic institutions · 108
academic probation · 79
Academy · 104, 105, 106, 107, 137
acceptance · iv, 78, 168, 213
acceptance speech · 78
accidental · 84
accolades · 214
accomplishments · 214
accountable · 262, 263
accuse · 126
accused · 43, 137, 141, 144, 263
achieve · 86, 149, 253
achieving · 164
aching · 53, 128
acquaintances · 150, 172
active · 226, 256
activism · 153, 184, 236
activist · 184
activities · 177
activity · 84, 208
addressing the role · 224
administered · 49, 231
administration · 16, 109, 176
administration's · 16
administrators · 16, 53, 116, 127, 157
admission · 72, 144

admitted · 99, 138
admonished · 118, 144, 197
admonishes · 209
admonishment · 215
adolescence · 205
adolescent · 23
Adroitly · 163
adultery · 207
adulthood · 205
adults · 21, 146, 174, 215, 261
advanced · 45
advances · 252, 253
adventure · 40, 47, 195, 236
adventurer · 160
advertisement · 109
advertising business · 197
advice of counsel · 152
affected · 26, 45, 188, 218
affection · 213, 214
affirmations · 28
afford · 9, 61, 117, 152, 194
Afghani · 177
Africa · 87
After Dinner Speaking · 104
afterlife · 248
age of enlightenment · 126, 175
age of ignorance · 167
age of information · 71
age of innocence · 103
agency · 58, 60
agenda · 69, 108, 133
agendas · 71, 138
agents · 141, 142, 143
aging · 246, 254
agog · 219
agonizing · 99, 129
ahead of time · 60, 81
aid · 42, 59, 61, 62, 64, 67, 74, 226
Aid · 57
AIDS · iv, v, 7, 11, 31, 33, 34, 35, 44, 57, 60, 61, 63, 68, 69,

71, 73, 76, 87, 91, 92, 94, 95, 97, 113, 114, 119, 124, 125, 130, 132, 171, 214, 215, 218, 224, 226, 227, 229, 232, 235, 255, 256
air conditioning · 160
Air Force · v, 6, 72, 78, 79, 84, 103, 104, 105, 136, 138, 140, 142, 147, 148, 149, 153, 165, 173, 185, 186, 187, 188, 190, 191, 196, 214, 253, 254
Air Force Academy · v, 6, 72, 78, 79, 103, 105, 106, 147, 148, 149, 165, 196, 214, 253, 254
Air Force major · 105
Air Medal · 137
Air Medals · 187
airborne · 139, 188, 189, 191, 194
aircraft · 84, 185, 187, 188, 191, 193, 194
aircrews · 142, 194
airflow · 188, 193
airframes · 185
airplane · 185, 188
airport · 161
airspeed indicator · 193
aisles · 22, 109
alcohol · 225
alcoholic beverages · 57
alien · 10
alive · 20, 54, 96, 152, 199, 206, 208, 227
Allan Ginsberg · 160
alleged · 141
allowed · 3, 42, 68, 70, 77, 89, 107, 126, 129, 142, 146, 167, 181, 208, 230, 261
Alpha waves · 72
altered state of consciousness · 224

B

309

counselor · 121
counterargument · 126
counterproductive ·
188
country · 17, 59, 80,
108, 109, 116, 121,
137, 138, 139, 142,
149, 152, 154, 155,
168, 179, 188, 217,
231, 254, 262, 263
county · 59
courage · 11, 215, 263
court martial · iv, 12,
159, 167, 214
Court Martial · 135
court-martial · 6, 135,
153, 252
court-martialed · 136,
255
courtroom · 154
courts · 174
cover up · 153
Covering · 163
covet · 168
Cowardly Lion · 29,
34
cowboy · 89, 219
cowboy boots · 89, 219
cowboy hats · 89
crack · 7, 34, 225
crave · 225
crazy · 39, 133, 150
create · 45, 72, 121,
137, 202, 251, 253,
255
creatinine · 229
creation · 203
creative · 84, 85, 173,
236
Creator · 71
credence · 113
credentials · 159
Credible Cat · 138, 151
creedo · 218
crescendo · 100
crew · 105, 185, 186,
192, 195
CREWMEMBER · 185
crews · 185, 187
cried · 78, 79

crime · 22, 120, 125,
140, 141, 144, 146,
148, 150, 153, 174,
252, 254
crimes · 146, 148, 151,
208
criminal · 147, 208,
261
crippled · 114
crises · 247
crisis · iv, 5, 16, 87
criterion · 151
critics · 126, 210
crosshairs · 165
crowd · 46, 48, 70, 220
crown heads of Europe
· 90
crucial redeeming
element · 217
crucible · 121
crucifixion · 166, 210
cruel blows · 131
Crunchberries · 22
crusade · 70
crushed · 173
cry · 46, 129, 167, 169
Crystal Light Corp · 23
cuffs · 36
cultural naiveté · 69
culture · 153, 160, 164,
252
cumbersome · 87, 213
curative substances ·
94
cure · 71, 90, 99
cured · 74, 168
cures · 90
curiosity · 114
curious · 78, 97, 207,
208, 209
curious phenomenon ·
246
currency · 252
curses · 207
curve · 79
cushion · 192
custody · 200
custom · 162
cycles · 162, 163
cyclical nature · 163

D

Dallas · 95, 217, 219,
236
damage · 138, 140
damaged · 118, 138,
165, 198
damaging · 250, 263
dance · 54, 235
dances · 219
Dane · 76
dangerous · 67, 125,
137, 151, 199, 216,
223, 226, 256, 262
dangerously · 115
dangers · 121, 137,
225
Daniel · 47, 236, 237,
239, 240, 241, 243,
260
dark and scary · 256
darkness · 78
Dateline · 6
daughter · 198, 207,
208
daughter-in-law · 207
daughters · 150, 207
daunting · 80
David Mixner · 136,
150
daydreaming · 76, 252
dead · 15, 209
dealership · 180
dealing with · 53, 78,
218
dealt with · 114, 205
Dean's List · 104
death · v, 3, 51, 77, 78,
81, 97, 111, 120,
130, 172, 174, 180,
182, 196, 207, 208,
226, 248, 263
death penalty · 208
debacle · 175
debate · 104, 169
debates · 199
debilitated · 131
debilitating · 43, 198
decay · 202
decaying orbit · 123

elitist institutions · 249
emaciated · 7, 52, 101,
132
email · 28, 176
embarrassed · 6, 251
embarrassing · 213
embarrassment · 41,
152
embittered · 197
embraced · 6, 13
emergency · 9, 12, 32,
42, 61, 64, 96, 122,
158, 174, 181
emergency room · 9,
12, 32, 42, 61, 64,
122, 181
Emergency Room · 16,
61
emotional agony · 131
emotional carelessness
· 224
emotional outlook ·
113
employed · 262
encouragement · 144
encroachment · 161
end of the line · 89
end-all-be-all · 255
endearingly insane ·
197
endeavor · 84, 174,
184
endeavored · 79
endless corridors · 96
endless discomfiture ·
97
endure · 7, 255
endures · 174
enemies · 189, 210
energy · 7, 43, 77, 160,
172, 201, 202, 203,
204, 246, 247, 255
enforce · 116, 209
engineering · 79
engines · 83, 84, 193
England · 173
English · 79
engrossed · 213
enhance · 72

enjoyed · 6, 13, 35,
108, 115, 164, 247,
261
enlarged prostate · 115
enormity · 198, 205
enormous · 129, 169,
181, 201, 203, 204,
219, 224, 252
enormously complex ·
180
enthralling activities ·
214
environment · 69, 107,
119, 188, 252
epidemic · 124
epilogue · 159
Episcopalian Bishop ·
162
Epzicom · 51
equal · 85, 164, 175,
177, 179, 189, 202,
218, 252
equality · 164, 174,
183
equations · 189
equipment · 105, 219
era · v, 69, 76, 163,
164, 174, 261
error on God's part ·
205
escape · 132, 152, 194,
199
eschewed · 249
Eskimos · 43
especially · 20, 63, 78,
87, 120, 142, 152,
154, 226, 254, 263
especially when it
hurts · 154, 226,
254
estate · 217
ether · 223
ethic · 217
ethically-oriented · 197
ethics · 263
ethnocentricity · 69
Eurasia · 162
Europe · 98, 162
evaluation · 135
evidence · 136

evident · 121, 172,
215, 219, 251
evil · 15, 100, 167,
208, 250
evil influence · 167
evil thing · 100
evils of homosexuality
· 121
exam room · 42, 114,
118, 158
exam rooms · 51
examination · 8, 37, 44
example · 17, 25, 27,
31, 59, 60, 62, 64,
104, 107, 150, 165,
175, 209, 213, 231,
263
excavating · 80
excavation · 80
excellent · 6, 16, 25,
30, 45, 59, 64, 68,
74, 255
exception · 41, 127,
187, 198, 210, 236
exceptional · 127, 198
excess fuel · 190
exchanged · 253
excitability · 135
excitement · 186, 219
exciting · 224, 253
exclude · 150
excluding · 137
excommunicated · 209
excruciatingly · 256
excuses · 218
executed · 121, 207,
208
execution · 120, 167
executive order · 167
ex-gay · 249
exhausted · 75
exist · 78, 126, 165,
202, 203, 204, 205
existence · iii, 3, 18,
114, 158, 166, 174,
195, 205, 206
exotic supplements ·
91
expenses · 60, 65
experience · 3, 5, 6, 8,
15, 18, 58, 68, 72,

G

inventory · 185, 186
invest · 77, 246, 247
investigation · iv, 149
invisible · 68, 158
invitation · 176, 227
involuntary · 46, 249
IQ test · 113
Iraq · 116, 126, 166, 197
iron · 202
ironic · 180
ironically · 167
Ironically · 138, 161
ironies · 137, 148
irony · 149
irrational · 7, 166, 175
Islamic · 166
Islamic fundamentalists · 166
isolated · 247
isolation · 245
Israel · 208
issue · 72, 78, 118, 122, 145, 169, 181, 205, 215, 216, 232, 233, 256
issues · 3, 60, 68, 115, 116, 126, 144, 180, 183, 233
itching · 43
IV · 132

J

jabbed · 198
Jack · 151, 153, 160, 173
Jack Kerouac · 151, 153, 160
Jalapeno · 26
James Bond · 15
Jamieson · 12, 17, 29, 31, 32, 33, 36, 42, 52, 116, 117, 118, 119, 131
JANUARY · 49, 67, 75, 95
jealous · 22, 161

jealously guarded · 261
Jerry Falwell · 165
Jesus and the Shamanic Tradition of Same Sex Love · 162
Jew · 145
Jim Bath · 159, 161
Jim Jones · 126
Jimmy Swaggart · 207
John Shelby Spong · 162
John Wayne · 35
joints · 128, 173
joke · 50, 105, 109
jokes · 29, 30, 107, 109, 246
joking · 140, 231
journal · v, vi, 3, 236
journey · 7, 18, 42, 90, 131
journeys · v, 124
joyous · 22, 255
JR's · 219
judge · 120, 136, 151, 204, 207
judgment · 218, 224
judgmental · 200
July · 111, 113, 114
June · 111, 138, 140, 141, 144
junior · 104
jury · 136, 144, 149
Just do it · 108
just government · 262
justice · 138, 147, 152, 179, 210
Justice Anthony Kennedy · 174
Justice Department · 176
justification · 146
justify · 145, 148, 164, 166, 168

K

Kaletra · 128

Kansas · 58, 89, 217, 246, 247
Kansas City · 89
keep it short · 218
Keith Meinhold · 136, 139
Kenji Yoshino · 163, 164
kidney pie · 229
kidney transplant · 115
kidneys · 114, 115, 116, 118, 122, 127, 128, 157, 158, 173, 229, 232, 237
kill · 71, 72, 121, 126, 187, 204, 208, 209, 255
killed · 12, 80, 208, 216, 256
killing · 7, 108, 120, 206
kind · 3, 12, 13, 19, 24, 29, 40, 46, 61, 77, 101, 129, 151, 158, 181, 198, 217, 226, 233
kindness · 30, 158
kiss · 220
KKK · 175
knots · 190, 191, 192, 193
knowledge · 72, 195, 205
KoolAide · 23
Ku Klux Klan · 175
Kyle Rice · 249

L

lab report · 43, 44
lab work · 32, 34, 42, 43
Labouchere Amendment · 173
lack of care · 181
lamenting · 248
Lance · 237, 241, 242, 243
landing · 142, 188, 193

ocean waves · 85
October · 10, 235, 245, 248
odds against it · 205
Odyssey · 95
offensive · 70, 71
officer · 39, 50, 107, 141, 142, 151, 191, 214
officers · 36, 147, 148
oil · 16, 90
old fart · 173
Old Testament · 209
older people · 172
older version of myself · 173
old-west · 89
Olestra · 22
Omni magazine · 253
on my behalf · 231
On The Road · 151
on the verge · 33, 129, 253
on top of · 31, 254
once and for all · 255
Onion · 25
online · 11, 114
open-mindedness · 91
operation · 115, 117, 118, 119, 157, 158, 235
operational · 197
operator · 47
opinion · 106, 174, 225
opportunistic · 114, 115, 118, 181
opportunistic illnesses · 114, 115, 118, 181
opportunities · 61, 65, 84, 86
opportunity · 45, 64, 109, 129, 173, 177, 215, 253
opposite directions · 188
oppress · 174
oppression · 105, 168
oppressively controlled · 109
optimism · 43

options · 44, 45, 63, 114, 122, 231
orbiting · 202
ordeal · 141, 144
order · 23, 50, 59, 84, 137, 142, 150, 167, 175, 184, 187, 188, 192, 202, 203
organizations · 59, 60, 61, 63, 64, 68, 122
original bang · 203
original explosion · 202
Orion · 77
Oscar Wilde · 173, 174
OSI · 141, 143
ostensibly · 100, 107, 143, 167
ostracized · 206, 208
other than we are · 223
ought not · 209
out · v, 8, 9, 12, 17, 22, 25, 27, 31, 35, 36, 41, 54, 59, 60, 63, 64, 65, 68, 69, 71, 73, 74, 77, 80, 81, 84, 86, 92, 96, 97, 99, 100, 105, 106, 107, 108, 110, 116, 119, 120, 121, 125, 131, 133, 138, 139, 140, 143, 144, 145, 147, 149, 150, 153, 154, 158, 159, 160, 162, 165, 167, 169, 172, 176, 177, 179, 186, 187, 191, 192, 194, 199, 203, 206, 208, 210, 214, 218, 219, 220, 223, 226, 227, 232, 233, 254, 255, 256
out of synch · 84
Out of the Past · 163
outdated and inaccurate · 186
outed · 6, 252
outlawed · 209
outlining · 253
outlive · 11, 76
outliving · 247

outlook · 81, 183, 247
outpaced · 216
outrage · 119
outside chance · 224, 255
outside limit · 191
overcast flight · 186
overrun · 193, 194
overwhelmed · 33, 220
overwhelming · 223
ownership · 169
oxygen · 202, 203
ozone · 219
Ozu · 195

P

Pacific Ocean · 188
pacifist · 263
pain · vi, 12, 21, 41, 43, 78, 96, 102, 111, 199, 246, 255
painful · 16, 49, 50, 74, 114, 127, 255
painless · 18, 38, 173
pajamas · 96, 99
pallor · 7, 172
Panama · 80, 186, 188, 189
Panama City · 188
pandemic · 31
panic · 157
paper flowers · 219
parade · 71, 219, 220, 227
parades · 154
Paradise · 49
paradox · 77
Paradoxical · 77
paradoxically · 210
Paradoxically · 18, 119
paralysis · 100
paralyzed · 100
parents · 54, 57, 63, 65, 69, 83, 154, 169, 172, 197, 205, 208
Parents Family and Friends of

Lesbians and Gays · 63
Parents, Family and Friends of Lesbians and Gays · 217
parishioners · 121
participants · 169
particles · 202, 203, 204
particles of antimatter · 202
particles of matter · 202
partner · 68, 130, 159, 197
passed away · 131, 133
passion · 6, 169
passionate · 179, 256
passionate intent · 179
pastors · 121
patience · 29, 37, 40
patient · 31, 36, 39, 51, 60, 118, 125, 128, 158, 229, 230
patients · v, 31, 33, 39, 51, 52, 60, 63, 73, 118, 119, 128, 129, 132, 181, 230
patriotism · 6
patron · 70
patronage · 35, 161
patronizingly · 169
pavement · 83, 193
pay over time · 230
payment · 159, 230, 231
PC · 261
peace · 86
peacetime · 187
Pecos · 58
pedestal · 214, 216, 218
peers · 76, 206, 247
penal swab · 37
penal swabs · 40
penalties · 147
penalty · 107, 208
pencil-pushing · 197
penis · 38, 135, 153
people are so mean · 256

perception · 3, 97, 223
perfect · 9, 254
perimeter · 193
perimeter road · 193
permanent · 77, 247
permanently · 101, 111, 113, 118
permeates · 165
permission · 108
perpetrator · 140
perpetuating · 223
persecute · 148
Persecute · 167
persecuted · 206
persecuting · 148
persecution · 146, 153
personal bias · 73
personal biases · 69
personal hardships · 199
personal loss · 197
personal property · 208
personal relationships · 237
personal revelations · 224
personalities · 199, 248
personality · 125, 185, 198
personality type · 125
personalization · 172
personhood · 214
perspective · 183, 197, 200, 208
perturbed · 92, 118
pervasive · 126, 162
perverse · 169
perverted · 205
petition · 161, 176, 177, 251
petitioners · 174
PFLAG · 6, 63, 135
P-FLAG · 217
P-FLAG · 219
P-FLAG · 220
P-FLAG · 227
pharmaceutical · 33, 35, 49, 64, 73, 181, 232
pharmaceutical companies · 64

Pharmaceutical Companies · 64
pharmaceutical generics · 65
Pharmaceutical Research · 51, 114
phenomenon · 19, 93, 161
philosophical · 67, 135
philosophy · 79, 149, 247
phone calls · 130
phones · 146, 262
phrase · 51, 144, 262
Phyllis · 76
physical condition · 113
physical exam · 43
physician · 7
physics of takeoff · 189
pickled herring · 168
pickup · 217, 219
pigs · 205
pill · 65, 73, 128
pills · 43, 45, 64, 73, 99
pilot · 138, 139, 143, 160, 190, 191, 192, 193, 195
pioneer · 254
pipe cleaners · 219
Pitrador · 30
pity · 11, 60
placebo · 51
plainclothes · 143
plane · 142, 190, 192, 193
planet · 65, 123
planets · 204
plans · 76, 81, 199, 230, 253
plastic sheeting · 219
plausible deniability · 262
play · 18, 21, 32, 40, 42, 78
playgrounds · 78
playing the field · 139
plenty to go around · 221

326

skids · 187, 189
skimmed · 194
Skinner · 252, 253, 254
sky is falling · 124
skyscrapers · 202
slaves · 167
sleep · 20, 43, 72, 73, 74, 85, 98, 100, 101, 140, 200, 207, 216
sleepless · 144
slides · 135
slow motion · 34, 193
slowed · 173, 194
small town · 246
Small, Still Voice · 171
small, still voices · 178
small-minded people · 173
smile · 32, 36, 40, 77, 132, 173, 205, 217, 256
smiling · 37, 76, 219, 220
Smith County · 115
smoke · 36, 43, 53, 83
smoker · 28, 35
smoking · 28, 53
snake oil · v, 90, 93
soaked to the bone · 221
soapboxes · 167
sobs · 129, 256
soccer · 249
Social Security · 9, 17, 60, 61, 62, 115, 232
Social Security Card · 61
Social Services · 17
social situations · 213
social worker · 9, 127, 159
Social Worker · 17
socialized · 165
socially unfit · 148
society · 148, 164, 206, 225, 252, 253
sodomy · 136, 141, 144, 147

solution · 70, 131, 165
solutions · 85
Sonic · 23
sons · 150
sordid past · 163
sore · 7, 127
sore throat · 7
sores · 10, 20, 43, 50
sorrow · 129
sorrowful · 114
soul · 19, 63, 154, 256
souls · 16, 90, 248
South American · 162
South Side Police · 199
Southern Christian Fundamentalists · 175
southern shore · 188
Southern sweet tea · 25
space · 253, 254
space colonies · 253
space technology · 253
Spanish Inquisition · 151
speakers · 219
Special Activities · 138
special consideration · 126, 127
Special Health Resources · 62, 128
specialist · 115, 127, 157
species · 80, 127, 204, 206
spectators · 169
spell · 100, 101
spirit · 31, 39, 45, 57, 86, 126, 173, 206, 247
spiritual · 28, 124, 131, 154
spiritually · 45, 65, 252
spit on · 206
sponge · 205
SPs · 192
squadron commander · 78, 79
squadron of the year · 78
squadrons · 105

SSA · 61
SSI · 61
stabilized · 99
staff · 33, 40, 51, 172
stage · iv, 40, 72
staging area · 219
stagnant · 80
stalled · 193
Stand By Me · 246
standard of conduct · 149
standoff · 126
stars · 77
startling · 80, 247
starvation · 7, 132
starving · 87
state · 7, 52, 59, 89, 114, 128, 150, 164, 168, 169, 174, 227, 230
state fair · 227
State-sponsored · 175
static · 85, 86, 203, 211
statistics · 79
STDs · 256
steal · 119, 263
steeped in tradition · 104
step dad · 33, 35, 36, 37, 40, 96
step-dad · 53, 58
Stephen King · 246
sterilizing · 148
Sterling · 247
still · i, 7, 20, 26, 32, 38, 54, 73, 76, 83, 85, 87, 88, 89, 93, 96, 97, 100, 101, 111, 113, 115, 116, 117, 119, 124, 128, 131, 136, 148, 151, 152, 158, 167, 171, 175, 178, 181, 194, 197, 208, 209, 210, 225, 235, 236, 253, 254, 256
stillness · 85, 263
stirs · 263
stockade · 83

talents · 198
tallies · 225
taste sensations · 22, 99
taught · 147, 148, 149, 153, 154, 195
tavern · 70
tax break · 116
taxied · 193
taxiway · 193
T-Cells · 44
teacher · 31
teachers · 169
teaching · 19, 71, 251, 263
teachings · 210
tears · 11, 12, 96, 145, 216
technically feasible · 189
technique · 30, 73, 74, 151
technological · 261
technologically · 252
technology · 71, 253
tedious · 169
telephone · 87
television · 97, 139, 154, 203
temper · 166
temperament · 197
temperature · 76, 96, 99, 188, 191
tempered · 186
tendencies · 205
tender · 246
tense moment · 190
tenuous · vi, 62, 114, 159
terminal · vi, 124, 196
terrain · 188
terrible · 54, 129
terrifyling · 247
terror · 100, 194
Terry · 217, 218
test · 11, 34, 35, 52, 54, 72, 81, 135, 230, 232
test audience · 246
testament · 12, 206

tested · 7, 9, 44, 70, 130
testify · 152, 224
testimony · 136
testing · 45, 72, 231, 232, 249
testosterone · 172
Texas · v, 11, 12, 16, 31, 36, 42, 50, 57, 58, 59, 61, 62, 65, 67, 75, 89, 99, 120, 121, 127, 128, 198, 217, 218, 219, 232, 245
Texas Dept of Health and Human Services · 61
Tex-Mex · 58
thankful · 20, 36, 40, 46, 54, 59, 78, 87, 97, 128, 195, 200
thanks · 34, 40, 127
The Advocate · 249
The Body · 246
the infinite randomness · 202
the system · 42, 158
theorem · 161
theoretical · 189
theory · 18, 161, 198, 252
therapeutic · 129
therapies · 31
therapy · 129, 237
Theta waves · 72
think · 6, 19, 37, 46, 61, 71, 76, 84, 92, 93, 95, 101, 105, 107, 119, 126, 127, 136, 137, 140, 144, 152, 155, 167, 171, 177, 179, 191, 198, 200, 203, 206, 218, 231, 254, 255, 262
think for yourself · 126
think freely · 200
thinking · iv, 8, 78, 91, 107, 127, 162, 165, 179, 201, 206, 236, 237, 251, 254, 262
thinking persons · 249

Those were the days · 167
though the cracks · 230
thoughtful reflection · 166
thoughts · 47, 73, 151, 152, 179, 197
threatens · 166
Three Moons Over Millford · 123
thrill · 224
thriving practice · 197
throwing stones · 210
thrush · 42, 64, 73
tightly knit · 186
tilt on the scale · 202
Tilt-A-Whirl · 46
time after time · 232
time machine · 47
time management · 104
time of day · 214
time over target · 189
timeline · 124
Tin Man · 30, 37, 38, 40, 42
tinfoil · 135
tires · 83, 193
to do nothing · 256
to take in stride · 196
toilet · 98
tolerance · 155, 168
Tolerance · 168
tolerated · 138
tolerating · 162
Tomatoes · 25
tongue-in-cheek · 176
too late · 86, 118, 138, 181, 199
top secret · 108
topic · 51, 91, 111, 149, 230, 231, 252
topography · 188
topping off the fuel tanks · 189
top-secret · 23
torso · 101
Toto · 30
tours · 108
tower · 190, 191, 192, 193, 195

unhappy · 215
unhealthy · 77
uniform · 105
uninsurable · 116, 117
uninsured · 117
unintelligible · 132
unique moment · 253
uniquely personal ·
131
united · 120
United States · 80,
103, 104, 106, 117,
167, 179, 180
United Way · 64
Unity · 65
universal · iv, 84, 161,
162
universal trait · 162
universally adored ·
160
universe · 201, 202,
203, 204, 210
Universe · 201
university · 63, 125
University · 31, 99,
114, 127
University of Texas ·
31, 49
unjust · 149
unjustifiable · 148
unjustly · 144
unkempt hair · 160
unlikely situation · 208
unmitigated · iv
unnatural · 209
unpatriotic · 263
unpleasant · 81
unpopular · 213
unprotected · 215
unqualified · 214
unresponsive · 96
unscheduled visits ·
139
unsuccessful · 174
untimely loss · 197
untreated · 42, 63, 130
unusual · 188
unworthy · 119, 250
upset · 245
upside down · 39, 146,
225

upturned · 215
urethra · 232
urgent · 7, 8, 9, 114,
132, 157
urgent care · 7, 8, 9
urges and behavioral
patterns · 224
urologist · 157, 158,
159, 181, 231, 232
USA · 59
USAF · 50, 197
USAFA · 108
useless · 76, 82, 100,
124
UT · 51, 52, *See*
University of Texas
UTHC · 127
utilities · 62
utilizing · 93
Utopia · 252
Utopian · 254
utterly alone · 10, 130

V

valence electrons · 93
valiantly · 32, 149
value · 10, 43, 63, 78,
128, 138, 172, 224,
226
valued · 198
valued and engaging ·
248
valueless · 250
values · 17, 19, 152,
166, 167, 207, 225,
262, 263
Van Nuys, CA · 52
vandalized · 140
variables · 188
VCR · 40, 142
vehicle · 109, 192, 194
venue · 70
verbal exchange · 215
vernacular · 190, 208
veteran · 6, 10, 116
veterans · 148
viable · 162
victim · 119, 120

victimless · 120
victims · 11, 147
Victor Powers · 151
victories · 110, 164,
255
victorious · 255
Viet Nam · 192
Vietnam · 148
viewpoint · 77, 250
Viginia · 89
vile · 209
vilified · 167
villages · 80
villains · 163
violation · 108
violence · 71, 121,
138, 165, 168, 206,
210, 252
violent · 168, 175
violent actions · 168
violent intent · 168
violently opposed ·
199
viral load · 44, 95, 128
virtually identical · 252
virus · 5, 19, 44, 73,
96, 180, 224
Visa · 58
vital · 26, 89, 223, 256
vivid dreams · 236
vociferously · 249
voice · 16, 38, 43, 98,
129, 171, 177, 178,
211
voicemail · 116
voices · 97, 98, 99, 178
volunteer · 150, 171,
196, 227, 235, 236
volunteered · 227
volunteering · 60
volunteers · 60, 117
vomit · 96
vote · 148

W

wait · 40, 42, 46, 62,
82, 101, 118, 173,

181, 191, 207, 230, 232, 254
waiting period · 115, 116, 117
waiting room · 29, 31, 33, 34, 35, 36, 37, 38, 39, 40, 42
wakeup call · 190
waking dream · 99
waking hours · 96
Walden Two · 252, 254
wall · 130, 177, 199
waltzing matilda · 49, 55
Waltzing matilda · 49
Waple · 144
war · 116, 126, 148, 167
warm temperatures · 189
warmth · 86, 220
warning signs · 52
warrant · 199
water · 24, 25, 96, 99, 248
waterproof · 221
waters · 194
waveforms · 84
weak · 7, 263
wealthiest · 116
wealthy · 69, 180
weariness · 98, 99
weary · 41, 98, 99, 169
weathered tree · 76
web · 60, 61
weep · 256
weight · 9, 100, 101, 154, 188, 194, 220
well · 9, 12, 13, 28, 31, 33, 45, 68, 75, 78, 87, 92, 119, 127, 133, 152, 162, 171, 172, 173, 176, 196, 225
well-adjusted · 250
well-being · 113, 137
wellness · 42, 44, 128
Wellness Center · 129
wept · 11, 149, 200
Wheel of Fortune · 36, 40

wheel-cap · 110
whispers · 100
white · 10, 37, 69, 70, 84, 85, 150, 154, 166, 171, 194, 211, 214
White Noise · 83
whiz kids · 187, 190
who is and who is not · 232
Wicked Witch of the West · 30
wickedness · 208
widow · 209
Will Roscoe · 162
William Burroughs · 160
willingness · 114
willpower · 129
Wilmington · 32, 67, 70, 159, 160, 161, 235
Wilmington, NC · 32, 67, 70
Wim Wenders · 78
win · 47
wind check · 193
wind conditions · 190
windscreen · 194
wine · 68
wing surface · 188
wings · 187
Wings of Desire · 78
winter · 99, 107
wiretapped · 146, 262
wisdom · 82
wish · 20, 82, 86, 87, 131, 168, 179, 235, 255
wishes · 86
witch-hunting · 152
witch-hunts · 138
withdrawal · 129
without the consent of any court · 176
witness · 151, 154
witness stand · 151
witnesses · 137
wives · 169

Wizard · v, 29, 31, 40, 41, 42, 43, 44, 51, 52
Wizard of Jamieson · v, 29, 40, 41, 42, 51
woke · 7, 72, 75, 95, 99, 103
women · 148, 149
wonder · 19, 37, 72, 76, 91, 122, 159, 205, 207, 209, 232
wonderful · 23, 28, 199, 220, 221
wonders · 114, 131, 247
wondrous · 46, 78, 255
woods · 83
word for word · 126
work · iv, vi, 9, 24, 27, 54, 60, 71, 92, 93, 114, 119, 125, 132, 145, 150, 171, 196, 205, 215, 227, 235, 236, 252, 253, 255
work-credits · 252
workers · 80
working · 105, 114, 189, 198
world · v, 21, 24, 47, 63, 83, 87, 99, 109, 124, 125, 154, 160, 165, 166, 168, 173, 179, 184, 195, 197, 199, 200, 202, 204, 206, 213, 247, 252, 253, 254, 256, 261, 262
world premier · 109
World Trade Center · 166, 175
worldly responsibilities · 124
worry · 37
worrying · 183, 248
worse · 79, 81, 90, 145, 147, 177, 182, 225, 252, 254, 255
worse for the wear · 249
worst pain · 255

To comment on this book, go to

www.lulu.com

www.amazon.com

www.barnesandnoble.com

or all three!

Visit my website at

www.tridd.com

www.ingramcontent.com/pod-product-compliance
Lightning Source LLC
Chambersburg PA
CBHW030413100426

42812CB00028B/2936/J